Association Britannique de la Garde Imperiale.

Publication 1: Napoleon's German Artillery

First published 2010 by Lulu.com. No part of this publication may be reproduced without the written permission of the author.

Acknowledgements,

I would like to thank all those who have assisted in the writing of this book. The book was written in 2006 as a follow up to the authors 'Napoleonic Artillery' which was a collaborative effort between Dr S Summerfield and Mr A L Dawson Bsc Hons.

I am indebted to S H Smith for the use of the illustrations from his private collection, as well as David Hollins, Ewe Ehmke, Digby Smith, Hans Karl Weiß, Oliver Schmidt, Dr M Kloeffler, Tony Broughton and no doubt many others whose names escape me. Too all who helped I offer my hearty thanks.

Paul L Dawson

Wakefield November 2006.

Table of Contents

Introduction..9
Chapter 1: Artillery of the Confederation of the Rhine.............13
Chapter 2: Use of Artillery..17
Chapter 3: Development and use of Horse Artillery................27
Chapter 4:Baden..48
Chapter 5: Bavaria..51
Chapter 6: Hesse-Darmstadt......................................95
Chapter 7: Kleve-Berg..111
Chapter 8: Mecklenburg Schwerin................................121
Chapter 9: Saxony..123
Chapter 10: Westphalia..145
Chapter 11: Württemberg..151
Glossary1: Organisation..175
Glossary 2: Ordnance..178
Bibliography..183

Introduction.

Napoleon Bonaparte, one of the most famous Europeans of the last millennia was a born gunner. His cannon were truly his *Ultimo Ratio Regum*. He used his guns with a calm, sure skill, improving his techniques from campaign to campaign. Napoleon has passed into history was one of the greatest civilian leaders and military captains.

This work aims to trace the evolution of the field guns used by Napoleon, and those of other nations involved in the Napoleonic wars. It will also show the impact of the 18th century arms race, a result of the various European and international conflicts of era, aided the development of muzzle loading black powder artillery in Europe and America. This arms race saw the change from the slow and lumbering, immobile artillery of the 17th century in to mobile and lightweight artillery, which would become a battle winning weapon rather than static infantry support. These new guns, developed during the 18th century were the corner stone of the tactics of the Napoleonic wars. As the guns evolved so did the philosophy about the usage of the guns, championed by the Austrian General Smola, and Emperor Napoleon.

The Revolutionary and Napoleonic Wars which swept through Europe between 1792 and 1815, saw the small professional armies of the Eighteenth Century quickly gave way to large national armies composed principally from conscripts. This same period saw artillery transformed from a specialised profession into a major service branch of the army, which became capable of dominating battlefields. An example of this is the French Army of Italy had in 1796 only 60 artillery pieces. Yet sixteen years later, at the Battle of Borodino, the artillery for both sides totalled some 1,200 guns and fired an average of 15000 rounds *per hour* during the course of the day's fighting on just two miles frontage.

Many factors combined to bring about this fundamental change; decades of technical improvements, improved higher level tactical doctrine and the rise in status of artillery officers. But how exactly was artillery of this period employed? How did it function during the confusion of combat? And most of all, what factors led to the rise in status of artillery from a belittled specialist branch to that of a new god of war? With this book the author and his collaborators aims to describe these changes.

The work is laid out so that the changes to the artillery system of each country is in chronological order, so that the reader may observe how the evolution of the artillery of one country affected that of their neighbours, in an arms race, and how campaign experience effected the development of artillery.

This study of the field artillery of the Napoleonic wars, does not just cover the Napoleonic Wars 1792-1815 as by necessity many of the field artillery systems used in the Napoleonic wars were conceived and put into operation over a half century before the conflict began. The study is half technical in nature, the first part is a survey of artillery tactics and the philosophy of artillery in the age of the great Gunner-Emperor, Napoleon. The second part details the major artillery systems of the period,

The Napoleonic Wars were the age of the artillery battle, with artillery organisation, employment, command and control as well as the guns themselves being constantly improved from 1805 by the major nations involved. The period also saw a great increase in the number of guns used, and saw a new brand of offensive artillery tactics develop. The gunners of all nations upheld the honour of their arm in the many campaigns fought to maintain oligarchs on their thrones, to protect Britain's self proclaimed right to control world trade and to maintain the balance of power in Europe against the ideals of the French Revolution and Napoleon.

Terminology

In this work, for ease of understanding,

- A battery refers to a tactical unit upon the battlefield although this term was not in common use until later in the 19th Century.
- Gun tube is also used to refer to the barrel of the cannon which is given in metric measure, and bore length which is given in calibres [i.e the number of calibres that would fit in the bore of the gun tube, calibre being the diameter of the bore].
- In order to produce consistency in weight and measure, the native units have been converted into metric to ease comparison between the artillery of each nation. So for example a French 6inch howitzer is in fact a 6.32 inch howitzer and a 5.6inch howitzer is in fact 5.7.2 howitzer, which is also referred to as a 24-pdr howitzer. France was the only country which referred to the weight of shot for howitzers in metal weight rather than the stone weight used in the rest of Europe, so a French 16-pdr howitzer is the same as an Austrian 7-pdr howitzer when one looks at the unit of measure used. The use of both a calibre measure and weight of shot measure had lead some authors to assume that the 1808 24-pdr howitzer was different to the 1808 5.72inch howitzer when they are inf act the same weapon.

Chapter 1: Artillery of the Confederation of the Rhine.

Caught between Prussia and Austria, both of which constantly seized every opportunity to ingest them, the smaller German states had increasing difficulty maintaining their independence. When the Austrians invaded Bavaria in 1805 without a declaration of war, ordering the Bavarian Army to submit to Austrian command, Bavaria, Baden, Württemberg, and Hesse-Darmstadt at once joined Napoleon. This alliance was formalized on 12th July 1806 when sixteen south and central German states seceded from the ancient Holy Roman Empire (no longer Roman and certainly never holy) to form the Confederation of the Rhine, with Napoleon as its "Protector". Other states joined during 1806-1808, bringing the total to thirty-five.

Each state pledged a military contingent in case of war. (France, in turn, pledged 200,000 men to the common defence.) A few of the tiniest states were allowed to substitute cash contributions.

Originally, the armies of these states differed greatly in organization, armament, training, and efficiency, many being cumbersome 18th century-type formations. Service with the French, especially against Austria in 1809, led to the adoption of French organization, tactics, and insignia. Through Napoleon's demands after 1808 for men for his grueling war in Spain caused resentment, the Confederation troops were loyal and usually efficient allies through the disastrous 1812 campaign. During 1813 they fell away, readily including Napoleon's borther in law Murat or regretfully.

Some allies stood by Napoleon to the end, Poland the Kingdom of Italy being the most notable.

In 1814, Prussia, Austria, Britain, and Russia combined to drive these states and their leaders, willingly or reluctantly, into battle against Napoleon. But something of an emotional tie - memories of hardships endured together, of battles lost and won - remained. After Waterloo, Napoleonic exiles often found safe haven in various German states. With the retreat of the French forces - except for the garrisons of several communications centres, some of which held out to the end of the fighting - after Leipzig the states of the former Confederation of the Rhine were summoned to join the Allies. Their responses varied. In the north, Mecklenburg-Strelitz,

Mecklenburg-Schwerin, the Saxon duchies, Lippe, and portions of Westphalia made real sacrifices to raise troops and money. By contrast Oldenburg contributed nothing; Hanover showed little zeal; its former ruler, returning from his English refuge, had quickly proven reactionary, incompetent, and unpopular. Brunswick expressed much good will, but was slow to muster troops. The Elector of Hesse-Cassel, once restored to his former capital, did find a few soldiers, but devoted more energy to restoring everything to its 1805 status, including large pigtails -on his officers and officials. Hesse-Darmstadt and Nassau (which the Prussians were busy plundering) dragged their feet, as did Baden. Bavaria stood stiffly on its Napoleon-bestowed status as a Kingdom; it finally provided 30,000 men, but kept part of the territorial gains it had acquired, 1805-1809. Württemberg following the battle of Leipzig in October 1813 was flooded with Austrians and looted in the slovenly Austrian style. Uncowed, its fat king sent only a few regulars (commanded by his Napoleon-hating son) to the Allies, and prevented the mustering of volunteer or Landwehr units. Saxony, Frankfurt, and Berg were put under direct Allied rule and stripped of men, money, and supplies.

In addition, the German states had to "support" the Allied armies, which had large appetites and brought little with them except typhus and "malignant dysentery". Only Wurzburg, whose ruling house was related to the Austrian Hapsburgs, escaped this exploitation.

In 1815 all these states furnished at least small contingents during the Hundred Days. The Saxons, placed under Prussian command, mutinied, and had to be "sent to the rear".

Chapter 2: Use of Artillery.

The artillery of the confederation of the Rhine, and of the major powers in the epoch was limited to a few but important roles.

Battalion and Regimental Guns

In the 18th century it was considered best practice to attach one or two guns to each infantry regiment. This system lingered into the early 19th century, and was enshrined in Russian doctrine until 1813 and Prussian doctrine till 1812. The majority of the Rhinebund states artillery was purely deployed at battalion level for close support of the infantry regiments the guns were assigned to.

Austrian Organisation.

Most states prior to entering into the Rhinebund organised their battalion artillery after the manner of Austria. In Austria, the line infantry battalions up to 1808 were supported by their own guns in the same manner as the Russian manner, after which the guns were taken away from the infantry and placed in to field batteries. These field batteries would accompany the respective infantry formation, much as did the French field batteries assigned to a corps or division[1], and would camp,

---
1 Hollins D 2005 pers comm

fight with their parent infantry formations. The battery could be subdivided into half batteries if the situation required to do so. Tactical doctrine established that the battalion guns were to be placed at the front of the infantry to bombard the enemy line, and as soon as the advance was ordered the guns in the first line moved to the intervals between the battalions and loaded with roundshot. These pieces advanced forward with the infantry by bricole, until the line had come within 500paces of the enemy when they were to begin to fire again, and were to continue to fire as long as the battalion to which the guns were attached were engaged with the enemy. The fire was to be continuous without any intervals. The guns were also to continually advance upon the enemy, and would change to case shot by 100paces, and with a few salvo's of case shot at close range, the action would be in favour of the Prussians. The regimental artillery attached to the second line was only to start firing if the first line was defeated and retreated through the second line. [2]

Until 1808, the line Infantry battalions were supported light battalion guns manned by a combination of gunners and unskilled labour provided by their Infantry regiment. The allocation of the guns depended on the terrain and likely

---

[2] Nosworthy B (1990) *The anatomy of Victory. Battle tactics 1689 to 1763* Hippocrene Books New York.

opposition. Infantry Regiments in Italy, the Tyrol and the Grenzers were issued with six 3-pdr cannon per regiment. Those operating outside these areas were issued with 6-pdr instead.

French Manner.

Upon entering the Rhinebund, it appears that most states battalion artillery usage changed over to that used in France. Napoleon believed that both raw conscripts with no or little battle experience, as well as seasoned veteran benefited from close support from the artillery[3] which was a view shared by the Russian high command[4].

Whilst battalion artillery in Austria did serve to dissipate the artillery's effects [5], the same was not the case for France and her allies in 1809-1812. In Russia, each infantry company was to have ten men and two NCO's trained as gunners, so they could be sent to the battalion artillery. In France the organisation of these light guns, unlike Russia, was a separate establishment to the field artillery proper, and did not weaken this establishment and resulted in the French

---

3 Napoleon, Correspondence no. 15723, 31: 328-329 to Clarke Minister for War 29 May 1809
4 Zhmodikov A & Zhmodikov Y 2003 vol 1 + 2 opcit
5 Zhmodikov Y & Jhmodikov Y 2003 vol 2 opcit

infantry had dedicated artillery support, in addition to that at divisional level, which in effect freed up guns from infantry support to be used in larger, and higher level artillery formations.

Brigade Artillery.

The some of the Rhinbund states prior to entering the confederation of the Rhine, for example Hess Damrstadt and likely Württemberg abnd saxony, copied the Austrian artillery, and continued to use the old pool system of deplopying artillery, parcelling out individual batteries to brigades or divisions. While the individual batteries were well led, there was little coordination among them.

Austrian Brigade Artillery.

The remaining guns allocated to the reserve were organised into batteries that could either supported the advance guard, or in the main gun line. Light guns (3-pdr and 6-pdr) were allocated for battlefield support as required and the heavy guns already place in position at the commencement of the battle. The reserve held about one third of all guns. As a rule of thumb one gun per thousand men was kept in reserve for key attacks, especially Horse 6-pdr and some howitzers. The emphasis in battle was all three arms working together.[6] Established doctrine attached the light artillery (i.e. 3-pdr, 4-pdr or 6-pdr) to infantry brigades their being one artillery company per brigade, its primary role being the direct support of infantry by deploying on the flanks of the companies or in the intervals between companies, not more than 107-m forward of the front line of the infantry[7]. The limbers were to be placed behind the line, along with the caissons, the guns being moved by bricole and handspike. In battle the guns were to be prolonged forward as in the Austrian system, the two lead horses being detached from the limber team for this purpose.

Divisional Artillery.

Only those states with a large artillery contingent followed French divisional artillery concepts, these states were principally Bavria, Saxony and Württemberg.

French Divisional System.

During the Revolutionary Wars, the artillery of France used whatever artillery they had at their disposal wherever they needed it. Batteries were often distributed amongst the Infantry in a support role. Individual batteries might have

---
6 D Hollins 2005 Pers Comm
7 Zhmodikov A & Zhmodikov Y 2003 vol 2 opcit

more than one calibre of gun and had up to two howitzers. However, theoretically after 1800 every battery had 6 guns of the same calibre and two howitzers. A quick glance at the organisation of the Artillery for the Battle of Friedland (14th June 1807) however still shows the use of mixed gun batteries. It also became standard practice to assign at least one foot battery per Infantry Division and possibly a horse battery. Divisional artillery always comprised of 8-pdr or 6-pdr batteries, and Horse Artillery was generally assigned 6-pdr as well, but 8-pdr had been used up to 1808, and in the Guard even 12-pdr had been used as horse guns. The 12-pdr batteries were assigned on a Corps level in the artillery reserve. In addition, depending on the availability of equipment, the Corps reserve could contain a number of light foot batteries or horse batteries.

What was unusual was that the French Army, as part of Napoleons reorganisation of the army as First Consul into a modern Divisional structure created semi-autonomous artillery formations that were under the command of smart and aggressive young artillery officers

Distribution of guns in the Infantry Divisions was done on a regular and equal basis, two main considerations were:

A) It was necessary that the Infantry Divisions were not encumbered with an excessive quantity of heavy artillery which opposes the rapidity of movements by its transportation difficulties.
B) The heavy artillery should be judiciously distributed between the Infantry Divisions and the excess assigned to the artillery reserve of each army. These reserves, placed under the immediate authority of the army commander in chief, can be employed with great advantage at the decisive moment of a battle.

Cavalry Divisions unlike those of the Infantry did not have permanently attached artillery. When required, Horse Artillery was attached from the Artillery Reserve. Sometimes Horse Artillery Batteries was assigned Cavalry Divisions or even Regiments that acted in the rearguards, advance guards or in the individual forces. Being the most mobile kind of artillery, Horse Artillery allowed it most rapidly concentrated in the necessary place significant fire power and therefore it very approached to the role of artillery reserve,

Positional Artillery.

Saxony was perhaps one of the few Rhinebund states with a large artillery establishment prior to the start of the French Revolutionary Wars and entry into the Rhinebund. Saxony, deployed its heavy 8-pdr and 12-pdr, and perhaps light 8pdr and 12-pdr in positional batteries.

When used to support an Infantry attack, the position battery would once again seek to obtain a position where it could fire into the opposing troop's flank. The closer the battery could get, the better- get up close and shoot quick was one French artillerists' maxim. However, this tactic required quick reactions to guard against sudden counter-attacks. To some extent the danger of this tactic could be overcome by leapfrogging batteries forward in alternate sections or by approaching behind a Cavalry of Infantry screen, and increased the surprise factor, which could often rout an in-experience enemy on its own.

18th Century Usage.

Frederick the Great considered heavy artillery as having a key role in assisting the infantry advance, and it was important not to let the guns fire prematurely. The opening rounds of a battery were the most effective, and the greatest resource at the disposal of the army commander. Timing of the opening salvo was crucial. Austrian doctrine of 1759 argued for the guns to open fire at musket ranges, as this was when the guns were the most effective, to hold the fire until that point. Prussian doctrine urged for the guns to fire by half battery in salvos rather than by single gun.

Position batteries were fixed position, and where ever possible sighted as to *enfillade* the enemies positions.

Austrian Position Batteries.

The Austrian manual suggested that a timber roof of light constructed be place over the gun to prevent the gunners from being injured by flying debris etc. From 1809 onwards, the Austrians tended to deploy their positional artillery in prepared field fortifications in the manner of Wagram and Aspern-Essling. The 1807 Austrian Kavallerie Reglement advocated that the infantry would advance supported by fire from the heavy position guns. A cavalry artillery battery would advance by half battery, the first half covering the fire of the second[8]. These batteries, once they had achieved their objective were returned to the artillery reserve, leaving the temporary field fortification as an obstacle to troops movement on the battlefield[9]. In exceptional circumstance

---

8 D Hollins 2005 Pers Comm
9 Ibid

would these position batteries be used offensively as at Lieberwolkwitz (October 1813), where two position batteries were advanced, by Oberst Stein to deny to deny the French troops a rallying point.

Reserve Artillery.

French Corps Artillery and Grande Batteries.
The development of mass artillery by uniting artillery divisions into a single Corps had an almost insurmountable obstacle in its way in the form of jealousy between divisional commanders. Fancy new ideas like Corps Artillery Tactics were all very well in theory but without its artillery a Division was vulnerable. Therefore, only in exceptional cases were Corps guns concentrated.. The Poles and Saxons never formed so-called grand-batteries as there were never enough guns to do so. In 1809 at Raszyn Poniatowski deployed 16-gun battery against the Austrians, in 1812 at Smolensk he set up 16-gun battery against the Russians. It was a far cry from the monstrous 220-gun Russian battery at Leipzig or the French 112-gun battery at Wagram.

Chapter 3:Development and use of Horse Artillery.

During the 18th Century there were a number of proposals and experiments aimed towards bringing field guns up quickly to the point of action. Generally, Frederick the Great is considered as the inventor of the Horse Artillery, although some claim that the Swedes and the Russians introduced Horse Artillery. Frederick adopted it to provide his advance guard support when it reconnoitred the terrain close to the enemy and to take the heights in front of enemy positions occupied by enemy Cavalry. To dislodge the enemy from these heights, he mounted the crews of an artillery battery, and ordered it to follow the advance guard, or another strong Cavalry command. These guns were used against the enemy Cavalry with great advantage, particularly when the cavalry had forced the enemy infantry to form square. Deploying just beyond musket range (approx 200meters), these guns could devastate the squares dense ranks with canister, 'get up close and shoot fast', was the doctrine of French General Maxamillien Sebastien Count Foy (1775-1825)[10].

---

10 Foy quoted in Laurema M (1956) opcit

There were three main systems in use
1. Prussian (horse mounted gunners)
   - Prussia 1760 +)
   - France (1792 +)
   - Austria (1759 – 1774)
   - Hesse-Darmstadt (1780's +)
   - Saxony (1780's +)
   - Baden (1806 +)
   - Westphalia
2. Austrian (vehicle mounted)
   - Austria (1774 +)
   - Bavaria (1785+)
   - France (experimental 1792-1800)
   - Württemberg (1808+)
3. Hanoverian (semi-vehicle mounted)
   - Hanoverian and Royal German Artillery
   - Württemberg (-1808)
   - France (experimental 1792-1800)

By the 1790's most European armies had introduced Horse Artillery. In General, Horse artillery was designed to get up close to an enemy body of troops, fire as many rounds into that body of troops in support of an attack and then evacuate the area as quickly as possible. As the horse artillery was generally working on much closer ranges than the foot artillery, it was deemed expedient to use small calibre guns (3-pdr), as they were light, and had a similar effect to a heavier calibre gun firing canister given the ranges involved.

By 1800 most horse artilleries were armed with 6-pdr, as they could fire larger doses of canister. The French took this idea to its logical conclusion and used 8-pdr and 12-pdr guns in their horse artillery. The decree of 29 August 1805 authorising the organisation of the Artillerie a Cheval of the Imperial Guard, stipulated that each of the 6 companies were to be armed with four 8-pdr, two 4-pdr and two howitzers.[11] In 1807 they were armed with six 12-pdr, twelve 8-pdr, ten 4-pdr, and eight 6inch howitzers.[12]

Prussian System (horse mounted).

In the Prussian system all the members of the battery were mounted. The teams of horses used to pull the guns had an additional pair, to increase the mobility of the battery, and to accompany the movements of the cavalry. The intention was to give the cavalry firepower, and to enable the artillery to seize high ground and defend it with the guns giving the

---

[11] SHAT Xab 57-59 Batteries
[12] "Situation du Material a 1er Mai 1807" cited in Lechartier (1907), *Les Services de l'arrirere a la Grande Armee*, p578-79).

impression that it was held by infantry. This ruse succeeded until Prussia's opponents became aware of this new style of artillery, in spite of Frederick's employment of this new weapon at decisive points in a battle, for example the battle of Reichenbach (1762)[13].

1759 saw Austria form her first horse artillery organisation after the defeat of the Prussians at Maxen on 21 November 1759. The initial horse artillery formation consisted of twelve 3-pdr drawn by two teams of four horses, in total 120 were needed. The first battery was ready for service in June 1760. The guns were deployed with the cavalry, and in the following year Russian horses and equipment formed a second battery of four 6-pdr for use in Silesia. These two batteries were still something of an experiment, and the horse artillery in Austria did no exist as a discrete branch of the artillery untill the 1770's and in a very different form to these first steps.

In 1785, the Marquiss de Lafayette (1757-1834) saw the Prussian flying artillery in the camp of Silesia in 1785, and began to extole its virtues in France, which initiated a protracted debate upon the virtues and limitations of horse artillery, and due to its significant cost in money and horses, nothing was done in France until 1792. Successes at Valmy

---

13 Mcconachy B opcit

(20 September 1792), Jemmapes (6 November 1792), enhanced the Prussian method of horse artillery due to its speed of movement compared to foot artillery.

From what has been said, it would appear that Prussian style horse artillery, able to deploy quickly, and to keep up with the cavalry, and to give the formations an element of solidity was the ideal type of artillery. However, horse artillery stripped the best men from the foot artillery, and was costly in one asset the horse. A horse battery had relatively small firepower compared to a foot battery (this was partially negated by arming the horse artillery with 8-pdr in the French army for a while), and presented a magnificent target to enemy artillery, infantry fire and cavalry attack, with its massed lines of horse holders, horses and caissons, often taking up more space than a foot battery because of the extended lines[14].

Paradoxically, the fully mounted artillery was slower to get into action. The mounted crew-members had to find themselves a safe spot to dismount before they arrive at their position, but they cannot leave their horses before the cannon has halted at the right position, the horse-holder has jumped down from the limber, and has walked to the horses to take

---

[14] Anonymous (1824) Observations sur les Changements Qu'il Paraitrait Utile D'apporter au Materiel et au Personnel de L'artillerie

over the reins. When limbering again, the cannon stopped until the crew has mounted again, and the horse-holder is then seated on the limber. Particularly in night surprises, fully mounted horse artillery was notoriously slow to move [15].

The disadvantage were [16]:-
> The mounted crew-members had to find themselves a safe spot to dismount before they arrive at their position, but they cannot leave their horses before the cannon has halted at the right position, the horse-holder has jumped down from the limber, and has walked to the horses to take over the reins. When limbering again, the cannon stopped until the crew has mounted again, and the horse-holder is then seated on the limber.

Austrian System (Vehicle Mounted).

The Austrians, who experienced the effectiveness of the Horse Artillery first hand from the Prussians, were the first to

---

15 Griffiths P (1976) *French Artillery*, Almark, Surrey
16 Hoyer J F (1798) Ueber die reitende Artillerie" Neues Militairisches magazin – Historischen und Scientifischen Inhalts, herausgegeben von Iohann Friedrich Hoyer, 1. Band, 2. Stück Leipzig 1798pp. 3-14 see also Hoyer J F 1802 Ueber den Gebrauch der reitenden Artillerie" by Von R., in Neues Militairisches magazin – Historischen und Scientifischen Inhalts, herausgegeben von Iohann Friedrich Hoyer, 2. Band, 4. Stück Leipzig pp. 10-14

imitate the Prussians and to make their army as effective as that of Prussia, which was regarded as one of the best army's in Europe. The first Austrian Horse Artillery crew was in action at Prague in the late 1760's, but the crews were not familiar with the characteristics of the Prussian Horse Artillery, and had to change the concept[17]. They realised, and this was confirmed by their experiments, that when the whole crew would be mounted, the guns [18]:

1. After reaching their position they could not open fire as quickly, as was the case when the crewmen would have been seated on the limbers.
2. That the huge amount of horses of the dismounted crew would give the enemy artillery a better direction to fire at, with a higher probability to score hits.

Therefore, the Austrian Horse Artillery was devised in such a way, that it would be able to reach easily and quickly every position were they would be necessary. The 6-pdr guns had a comparable carriage to the Prussian ones, pulled by a four-horse team. The crew was seated on the gun trail, longer then usual, the men positioned behind each other, with their feet on both sides of the trail on the ammunition chests. It was believed that the artillery would be able to advance this

---

17 Ibid
18 Hollins D (2005) Pers comm

way at the same speed as the Cavalry was marching. Proof, that the Austrian reached their goal to create a Cavalry-artillery completely is that this concept was unchanged up to the 1820's. The amount of shots carried on the limber was enlarged by adding two horses with pack-saddles to each gun. When in position, these horses were used to retrieve ammunition from the caissons, and form a reserve in case of an emergency. The crew consists of five men. The NCO was mounted and leading the gun [19].

The difference between both concepts is really striking. The Austrians were probably slower in their movement compared to the Prussians, but are serving the guns much quicker when deploying. Beside this, the only target for the enemy is the cannon itself with its crew, while with the Prussians the horses are added, not to speak about the enormous amount of horses that also had to be taken care off [20].

Hanoverian System (semi-vehicle mounted).

Shortly before the French Revolutionary War, (crica 1786) the Hanoverian army introduced the concept of Horse Artillery, then in common use in Europe. They copied the Prussian and Austrian systems, combining the advantages of

---
19 Hoyer 1798 Opcit, also Hoyer 1802 Opcit
20 Ibid

both. It was called the 'Geschwinde Artillery' ['fast artillery'] or "flying artillery". Initially, the Hanoverians utilised the 3-pdr weighing 600lb (273-kg) for their horse artillery. It was equipped like their regimental guns, and had a large ammunition chest carried on the limber in the Prussian manner. The limber wheels were also the same size as the carriage wheels, and the pintail used to hitch the gun carriage was replaced with a large hook, mounted directly on the wooden axel block [21].

This had the obvious advantage of making both gun and limber the same level, and making the gun carriage quicker to unlimber. The crew consisted of an NCO and eight gunners.

The NCO and four gunners were to be mounted; the remaining four gunners were vehicle-mounted; two were seated on the gun-carriage, and two on the limber ammunition chest. The gun and limber were drawn by a team of six "good" horses. The four riding horses of the mounted gunners could be used to augment the horse team to help draw the gun through soft ground or on bad roads.

---

21 Letter to W Congreve from J Saint-Ledger, Royal Artillery Institute Woolwich

When a gun was to be deployed, the crew dismounted behind the gun, with one gunner staying with the horses. The gun was unlimbered by the gunners seated on top of the gun-carriage.

The Hanoverian horse artillery were considered the finest and fasted in Europe during the revolutionary wars. This was due to the fact that with most of the gunners being vehicle mounted there were fewer horses involved and that it could be brought rapidly into action.[22] This semi-vehicle mounted artillery was copied in Württemberg and experimented with in France for a time as well .[23]

Usage of Horse Artillery.
Costs to maintain Horse Artillery were much higher then normal artillery, and used in the same way its effect would not be no different, so commanders sought to use the horse artillery in its most affective way possible, the tactics changing throughout the epoch. One major mistake in the handling of horse artillery was it use as regimental guns attached to the Cavalry which was a failing of the way in that Austrian Horse Artillery was deployed up to 1808.

---

22 Ibid
23 Strack von Weissenbach Opcit, also Smith D 2006 Pers Comm

Although the Horse Artillery was much quicker to deploy then normal artillery, it was still hampered by its vehicles, and obstacles caused by the terrain which could be difficult to pass, so that a solitary horseman from Cavalry that has been beaten always will outrun it.

Reserve Artillery.

When on a certain day, the commander in chief has already committed all other troops, the Horse Artillery, it was recommended, should form his last reserve. With its aid, the commander was able to put the crown on his victory, or to limit the results of defeat.

> *If, for example during a battle, because of bad deployment or by enemy fire, a gap appears in a wing or in the centre of the line, and the enemy threatens this part of the line with Cavalry or Infantry, or maybe already has broken into that part of the line. In this situation, (part of) the Horse Artillery, according to the circumstances, with its characteristic speed, can close the gap itself, or deploy at a favourable position near the threatened spot, to drive of the enemy with all power. For this purpose a part or all the Horse Artillery would have to be positioned in the vicinity of the*

commander in chief or the general in command of the artillery at the beginning of the battle.

In the same way the Horse Artillery would be used by the commanding general: to be able to reinforce every part of his line or position with guns at the utmost speed, as soon as it will become clear that the enemy would have a numerical advantage on that part, especially if this numerical superiority could have bad results. The Horse Artillery is very advantageous when pursuing the enemy, because it can leave one position, and deploy in another one very quick. At the same time, the enemy is suffering from its fire, pursued by the Horse Artillery the whole time, and prevented from occupying new positions. During retreats the Horse Artillery can give the same profit: Because of its characteristic speed and manoeuvrability it is able to cover the army by continuous fire from one position after another, and still following the own troops without being cut off.

1808 Prussian Horse Artillery Regulation

Manoeuvres in the presence of the Enemy.

With Horse Artillery alone, he was able to undo the results of mistakes caused by the terrain, by the forces at his disposal, by his subordinate commanders, or by his own doing. However, the Horse Artillery has to be treated as accordingly, as giving it a stationary position in the line, and treating it like all other artillery, means that its advantages were nullified, as well as depriving the commander from a very useful aid.

During all manoeuvres by units, executed at high speed and in full view of the enemy, which have to be supported by artillery, the presence of Horse Artillery was indispensable. No artillery was able to perform this task the way Horse Artillery could. For example when part of the army is outstripping the enemy, the Horse Artillery was able to relieve the task of the outstripping units enormously, by firing at the enemy from one position after another, and finally to enfilade and fire in the back of the outstripped enemy line. On the other hand, the Horse Artillery is able to prevent enemy troops from outstripping the own lines, by deploying quickly, and firing in the flank of the attacking forces. If the enemy line is defeated on one of his wings or in the centre, the Horse Artillery would be more efficient in supporting the troops that had to exploit the gains; because of its speed, it was able to complete victory moving from one position after another.

1808 Prussian Horse Artillery Regulation

Occupying favourable positions.

Using the Horse Artillery, the commander in chief was able to occupy speedily any unoccupied favourable position in front of or to the side of his own lines. He was even able to occupy such a position before the enemy could, by sending in several Cavalry squadrons, as many as the situation made necessary, supported by Horse Artillery. Together, the Cavalry and Horse Artillery would have been able to maintain such a position, until they could be reinforced by Infantry. During reconnaissance in force, the presence of Horse Artillery to protect a sudden retreat was indispensable: normal field artillery would only have been a hindrance during the reconnaissance.

1808 Prussian Horse Artillery Regulation

Supporting Cavalry Operations.

During an attack by the Cavalry on enemy Cavalry, the presence of the Horse Artillery would hamper the speedy and flexible movement of the Cavalry, which was of the utmost importance during such combats.

> *During 'invasions' of Cavalry, often executed in distant parts of the terrain and which have to be fulfilled with the utmost skills, the Horse Artillery was the most effective, in fact the only support. It was able to replace every kind of Infantry, without sharing their slow movement rate.*
>
> 1808 Prussian Horse Artillery Regulation

An example of Horse Artillery being used to support Cavalry operations was on 23 May 1793, the French were dislodged from Camp Famars. Robert Brown (a Coldstream Guards Corporal), wrote "An Impartial Journal of a Detachment from the Brigade of Foot Guards, commencing 25 February, 1793, and ending 9 May, 1795" was a spectator of this action:

> "The troops which displayed their valour and activity most, were the Hanoverian flying artillery, with the British light Cavalry, and those of the several other nations, as the nature of the engagements were chiefly adapted to their mode of warfare, in pursuing a flying enemy in an open country, where very few impediments occur to obstruct their progress. It was a glorious fight, as the morning was serene and

clear, to see the line of battle formed for an extent of several miles; in one lace squadrons of Cavalry charging each other in full career, in another the enemy flying and our's pursuing, with the flying artillery, displaying all the skill and dexterity peculiar to themselves; and the brigade of Guards was so situated in the morning, that they could behold almost the whole scene of action at one view."

Supporting Infantry.

In support of light Infantry, Horse Artillery has a large advantage where most operations are based upon speed, only to be executed by the Horse Artillery. No other artillery was able to execute such operations, and their speed is advantageous during the retreat, when they can support the retreating troops at the utmost.

During surprise attacks, which most of the time was executed on a grand scale and for which speed was a condition for victory, Horse Artillery was very useful to support Infantry as well as Cavalry. In case of failure, its speed is a big advantage in covering the retreat of the defeated troops, as well as to save themselves.

1808 Prussian Horse Artillery Regulation

Chapter 4: Baden

One of the original members of the Confederation of the Rhine, Baden was responsible for a contingent of 8,000. Its army had four infantry regiments, two cavalry regiments, a jäger battalion, a battalion of foot and horse artillery, plus the Grand Duke's guard. Much coached by Napoleon, the Baden troops - after mediocre service in 1805-1807 - developed into a tight, highly professional force on the French model and were much praised for their military qualities, even during the worst of the 1812 retreat out of Russia. Elector Carl-Friedrich is promoted to the rank of Grand Duke.

The artillery was raised in 1786 had 2 officers, 2 NCO and 32men manning 8x 3-pdr. In 1792 the battery had 3x 6-pdr and three 7-pdr howitzers. In 1803 the artillery had been re-organised, is strength increasing to 3x officers, 7x NCO, 54x gunners, 1x trumpeter, 71x train drivers, 145x horses, 20x caissons, and 10x wagons. The company was commanded by Major Strolze, Major Lux his predecessor taking command in the 1790's. It was armed with 6x 3-pdr.

On 1st May 1805, new guns were cast in Mannheim (Bavaria) to replace the 3-pdrs. On 1st October 1805 the company had

2x officers, 6x NCO's, 1x bonbardier, 1x drummer, 65x gunners and 6x 6-pdr guns.

By the 20th January 1806 the Baden artillery had 7x 6-pdr and 5x 7-pdr howitzers. On 1st November 1806 a horse artillery company was raised, being equipped with 6x 4-pdr guns of French origin. At this time their were three Foot Artillery companies each armed with 3x 6-pdr and 3x 7-pdr howitzers, being in total 14x 6-pdr, 6x 7-pdr howitzers and 6x 4-pdr. The number of guns was officially increased from 3x 6-pdr to 6x 6-pdr with an order of 4th October, evidently no new guns had been issued a month later.

Re-organsation of 1808:
- the 12pdr foot artillery (3rd) and half battery of horse infantry attached to the contingent destined for Spain. Arriving in Spain, the foot artillery had to exchange their 12pdr's for 6x 4-pdr field guns.
- The remaining 6pdr foot artillery battery and half horse artillery battery (according to Gill 2x6pdr +and 2x howitzer[24]) served in Europe (1809) and participated in the 1812 Russia

---

[24] Gill JH (1998), "Vermin, Scorpions and Mosquitoes: The Rheinbund in the Peninsular," In Ian Fletcher, *The Peninsular War: Aspects of the Struggle for the Iberian Peninsular*, Spellmount, Staplehurst, Kent pg 65-91.

campaign. In prapartion for the campaign of 1812, in 1811 two guns under Premierlieutenant Wild were sent with the 2nd Baden Inf. Regt. to Danzig. These were the only Baden guns which went to Moscow. They were lost at the retreat, near Smolensk. The officers of the regiment at the time were: The officers on service in Spain were as follow:

Major von Lassolaye (wounded)
Secondelieutenant Bender (died 1st february 1810 at Segovia)
Secondelieutenant von Fabert
Secondelieutenant Fülling
Secondelieutenant Kleiber (died 22nd august 1809 at Toledo)
Secondelieutenant Rückert
Secondelieutenant Schuhknecht
Secondelieutenant Schulz (died 28th july 1809 at Talavera)
Secondelieutenant Zeitler (diet 1st february 1810 at Segovia)
Secondelieutenant Hammes (Train)

The remaining 6-pdr foot artillery battery and half horse artillery battery (according to Gill 2x 6pdr + 2x howitzer) served in Europe (1809) and participated in the 1812 Russia campaign. I

The organisation remained the same until 15th March 1809 when each company was to have 8x 6-pdr, 4s 7-pdr howitzers, 16s 6-pdr caissons, 12s howitzer caissons, 22s infantry munition caissons and 14x forage wagons. The train had 382 men and 704 horses.

On 20th March 1811 a fourth foot artillery company was formed by taking guns and gunners from the existing three, returning the number of guns to 6x 6-pdr and two howitzers.

n prepartion for the campaign of 1812, in 1811 two guns under Premierlieutenant Wild were sent with the 2nd Baden Infantry Regiment. to Danzig. These were the only Baden guns which went to Moscow. They were lost at the retreat, near Smolensk. The officers of the regiment at the time were:

Capitaine 1st class Fischer
Capitaine 3rd class Sensburg (died)
Premierlieutenant Creuzbauer
Secondelieutenant Schwab (died)
Secondelieutenant Rummer
Secondelieutenant Wind

Secondelieutenant Swaab
Regimental surgeon Nußbaumer
Battalion surgeon Würthle
Premierlieutenant Petermann (train)
Secondelieutenant Hammes (train

Most the artillery was lost in Russia, son on 1st February 1813 two foot artillery companies were reformed, armed with 6x6-pdr and 2x howitzers, by 30th April 1813 this had increased to four foot artillery companies and one horse artillery company, a second horse company being raised in January 1814. The organisation remained the same until after the epoch.

Equipment

When first raised in 1786, Baden had one battery of 8x 3-pdr, changing to a battery of 6x 6-pdrs in 1803. Upon joining the Confederation of the Rhine, new guns were introduced according to the decree of April 14th 1806 which harmonised the calibre of artillery pieces in Europe.

Baden fielded only one battery of 6x 6-pdr during the 1812 campaign as regimental artillery for the four Baden Line Infantry Regiments, which was organised by the decree of 11th February 1811, and was issued 2x field guns, 6x caissons, 2x 7-pdr howitzers, 2x howitzer caissons, 4x infantry caissons, and 1x park wagon. The six guns were brigaded as a field battery with two howitzers, served by 64men. The guns were of French calibre, as issued when part of the Baden army served in the Peninsular. Apparently the foot artillery were armed with at least one 12-pdr battery, again of French calibre.

Baden lacked a cannon foundry so all guns appear to have been cast and built in Bavaria at Mannheim. The 6-pdr had a calibre of 103.5mm, was 18calibres long (1.86m), the 7-pdr howitzer had a calibre of 184.5mm and a bore length of 96cm.

In 1814 the artillery was armed with a mixture of French and Saxon guns. The artillery had the following guns:

16x Saxon 6-pdr, 6x Austrian 7-pdr howitzers, 6x French 6.32 inch Howitzers, 6x French 12-pdr, 6x French 6-pdr.

In 1815 all guns were harmonized to those of the French system, the guns being a 6-pdr, 12-pdr and 24-pdr (or 7-livre) howitzer. The siege artillery consisted of 16-pdr, 24pdr and 8, 10, and 12 inch Gomar chamber mortars. Batteries had 6 or 8 pieces plus two howitzers. Gun carriages and caissons were of the French Gribeauval principles.

In the 1820's an artillery committee was formed to overhaul the artillery equipment of Baden. All equipment up to this stage had been built on the French Gribeauval principals. Captain Ludwig was charged to examine the new systems of artillery then in use in Europe in order to improve the artillery of Baden in the most advantageous way possible, and proposed the wholesale adoption of the then current English system of artillery.

Baden Foot Artillery during the Peninsular War. (S H Smith).

Chapter 5: Bavaria

Bavaria was the most powerful state of the Confederation, with a contingent of 30,000 men. (When invaded in 1809, it put 47,000 men into the field.) Its Prince Elector Maximilian Joseph-promoted by Napoleon to Maximilian I, King of Bavaria, in 1806 - had worked to modernize Bavaria's army since his accession in 1799, organizing and training it on the French model.

In 1792 Bavaria consisted of the Electorate of Bavaria, Electorate of the Rhineland Palatinate, Zweibrucken, and the Duchies of Berg and Julich. In 1792, Bavaria mobilised under a commitment to the Holy Roman Empire against France but by October declared herself neutral. In 1796, diplomats from all the warring states met at the Congress of Ratstatt to redraw the map of Europe but before the treaty could be finalised war broke out again.

In 1799, Max Joseph succeeded his father as elector and allied herself to Austria. Since 1799, he had worked to modernise his army upon the French model ably assisted by Jakob Manson, a French émigré who had served in the French and Russian Artillery.

The Bavarians were Good combat soldiers with considerable dash and toughness, usually well-equipped and cared for, these troops did have certain characteristics that inspired the acerbic Prussian comment "Bavarians are the offspring of a man and a Austrian".

Nevertheless, Bavaria's troops were an important part of Napoleon's armies in both 1809 and 1812. The next year, sensing that the tide of war had turned, Maximilian gradually shifted to the side of the Allies in as dignified a fashion as he could manage - only to see his army run over and stamped flat by the retreating French at Hanau.

As a member state of the Holy Roman Empire, Bavaria was required to provide an armed force to fight for the Imperial cause in time of war. It was due to this commitment that Bavarian forces were mobilised to fight France in 1792 but by October that year she had declared herself neutral. In 1796 diplomats from all the warring states met at the Congress of Rastatt to redraw the map of the Empire. The result was strongly in favour of the French, as they had conquered Belgium (Spanish Netherlands) , Alsace, Lorraine and much of the left bank of the Rhine. Before the treaty could be finalised war broke out again and the French diplomats were murdered by the Austrians while in transit. The fighting ended with a French victory at the battle of Hohenlinden in December 1800. The result was a new carving up of the Empire with the free Imperial cities loosing their status and like many other small states, being incorporated into larger German states. Bavaria gained territory and the troops that went with it.

Artillery increased to regimental strength early on during this period and consisted of 2 battalions - the 1st or horse artillery battalion and the 2nd or foot artillery battalion. Each battalion had four companies of 150 men, six guns and two howitzers per company. Rank and file carried pistols and short swords with the foot artillery being issued muskets in 1811 while horse artillery had cavalry sabres. In September 1806 an artillery driver battalion established with a strength of eight companies, in total 1,062 men. Later 29th April 1811, the artillery is formed into a single corps, combining the light artillery, horse artillery, foot artillery and artillery train. By 1813 the Bavarian army had six 6-pdr batteries (two per division) and four 12-pdr batteries forming the artillery reserve.

Organisation.

During the 1790s the Bavarian army was reformed mainly due to the influence of the American Benjamin Thompson (later Graf von Rumford) who although mainly a chemist (and inventor of the coffee percolator) altered their uniform and introduced a new small artillery piece. In 1792 he was made a Count of the Holy Roman Empire, and he took the name of his old town American of Rumford. Our main interest in Count Rumford arises out of experiments he made five years later. His interest in field artillery led him to study both the boring and firing of cannons, his artillery designs were so highly regarded that by 1799 US President Adams tried to persuade him to return to America to found a Military Academy. Rumford introduced his own 3-pdr in 1795, and in the following year introduced Austrian gun tubes of 6-pdr, 12-pdr and 7-dr howitzer to replace the existing equipment.

On the 25th March 1800 the artillery regiment was founded with 9 "Bombardier-Kanonier" companies, 1 Horse Company and 1 "Ouvriers" Company. The bombardier-Kanonier companies were divided into three brigades, each of three companies. The first was commanded by a Lieutenant Colonel, the second by a Major, and the last by a second major. Each company was organised into eight single gun sections, two howitzer troops (bombardieren) and six field gun troops (kanonier-coporalschaften). The ouvriers were under the command of the Director of the Arsenals, and were separate from the artillery regiment, the organisation of the regiment being as follows[25]:

Upper Staff: 1 inhaber, General von Manson, 1 colonel, Baron Hallberg,
1 Lt Colonel, 2 Majors, 1 General Adjutant, 2 Regimental Adjutants.

Middle Staff:
2 quartermasters, 1 clerk, 1 senior surgeon, 2 junior surgeon.

Junior Staff:
1 gunsmith, 1 drum major, 1 provost, 1 jung.

Bombardier-Kannonier Company:
1 1st Lieutenant, 2 2nd Lieutenants, 1 senior pyrotechnician, 1 Fourier, 2 corporal junior pyrotechnicians, 6 corporals, 6 1st bombardiers, 6 bombardiers, 18 1st gunners, 18 2nd gunners, 32 cannoneers, 1 drummer, 1 probationary surgeon.

---

[25] Lutz 1894 p34

A field gun section was commanded by 1 corporal, 3 1st gunners, 3 2nd gunners and 4 cannoneers, the howitzer section was commanded by a corporal junior pyrotechnician, with 3 1st bombardiers, 3 2nd bombardiers, 4 cannoneers.

The ouvrier company, founded by Jakub Manson, based in the arsenal was commanded by a captain, and consisted of of 1 1st Lieutenant, 1 2nd Lieutenant, 1 sergeant-major, 1 Fourier, 5 corporals (1 black smith, 1 gun borer, 1 gunstock maker, 1 wheel wright, 1 carpenter-cabinet maker), 5 lance corporals, 6 smiths, 3 gunlock smiths, 1 nail maker, 2 gun borers, 6 gunstock makers, 7 wheelwrights, 1 latheworker, 4 carpenters, 4 cabinet makers, 1 drummer. The company was divided into four sections, one of wheelwright wagon makers, one of borers and gunsmiths, one of black smiths and one of cabinet makers. Each section was supervised by a corporal. The ouvriers were seected by the Colonel commanding the arsenal after he had inspected their work, their daily salary being 10 kreuzer a day. Advancement and promotion was at the direction of the inhaber and the commanding colonel subject to review by the Elector. In the same manner, the commanding colonel chose his staff and their appointments were approved by the Elector and Inhaber. Promotion of officers was dependant on their years of service and on the quality of their service records. The quartermaster was selected by the colonel, but given final approval only by the elector.

In total the regiment had 80 guns and 880men[26]

When an artillery artificer sergeant was due for promotion, he was subjected to an examination in three subjects prior to advancement. All bombardiers and cannoneers also underwent examination prior to advancement, which was initiated by the company officers, and approved by the Inhaber.

The artillery was inspected and reviewed by a War Commissioner every month. The arsenals of Bavaria were controlled by the Artillery Directory, which was organised as follows:

Munich: arsenal and powder mill, powder magazines of Grunwald and Inglostadt.

Amberg: cannon factory at Forschau and magazine at Rottenberg.

---

26 Lutz 1894 p33

Jacques Charles Manson, colleague of J b de Gribeauval and artillery engineer of France and Bavaria.

The Artillery Directory at the time consisted of Graf von Rumford, who returned to Bavaria in 1805, the Director General (Manson), the Adjutant General was Baron Zoller, the under director Colonel Comeau, and his assistant was Lt-Colonel Colonge; other members were the Swissman de Pirah. Swissman Lintz was appointed to take charge of the Ouvriers and had been a senior officer with Manson in the Armee of the Condee and was also a French Émigré officer.

In 1801 after defeat at Hohenlinden a year earlier, Bavaria changed sides and were given the free Imperial cities of Passau, Freising, Augsburg, Bamberg and Wurzburg.

In French Service.

The decree of 12th March 1804 required that the horse artillery brigade be differentiated in name from the Artillery regiment, and a commission was established to insure the serviceability of officers riding horses and consisted of a 1st Lieutenant, a quartermaster and a blacksmith. The horse artillery was disbanded on 14th March and distributed to the foot artillery. On 23rd March 1804, the artillery increased to regimental of 2 battalions (the 1st (Horse) Artillery Battalion and the 2nd (Foot) Artillery Battalion). Each battalion had four companies of 150 men each serving six guns and two howitzers. The organisation was as follows:

Staff: 1 Regimental Inhaber, 1 Colonel, 1 Lt Colonel, 3 Majors, 1 Adjutant General, 2 Regimental Adjutants.
Middle Staff: 1 regimental quartermaster, 1 regimental clerk, 1 regimental surgeon, 3 assistant surgeons, 3 probationary surgeons, 1 munitioner, 1 drum major, 2 provosts.
Company Officers: 6 Hauptman, 6 Captains, 11 1st Lieutenants, 22 2nd Lieutenants.
NCO'S and Men: 11 senior pyrotechnicians, 11 Fouriers, 22 Bombardier-Corporals, 88 Cannoneer-Corporals, 22 drummers, 132 1st bombardiers, 88 2nd bombardiers, 231 1st gunners, 462 2nd gunners, 704 cannoneers,

During wartime each company was increased with the addition of four more cannoner-corpoals.

In 1805, fought against the Austrians in Germany and the Tyrol. In 1806, gained the Tyrol, Voralberg, Brixen and Trent from Austria but lost Wurzburg to Grand Duke Ferdinand who relinquished Salzburg to Austria. The order of 28th September 1806 ordered the formation of the Artillery and Transport Battalions, each to contain eight companies, each to consist of:

> 1x Captain, 1x quartermaster, 1x senior smith, 1x adjutant, 9x lieutenants, 8x wachtmeisters, 8x Fourier, 32x corporals, 8x trumpeters, 16x smiths, 16x saddle makers, 960x drivers.

In 1806, Bavaria joined the Confederation of the Rhine. Bavaria was provided a contingent of 30,000 men. In 1806, LG and Chief of Artillery Jakob Manson reduced the companies to 100 gunners serving six guns to improve control. The organisation of the artillery for the 1806 campaign was as follows [27]:

---

27 Lutz 1894 p 43

1st Army Division.

Artillery commander Baran Gasoard de Colonge. Major Graf von Spreti

    1 Brigade: 6-pdr foot battery: Hauptmann Peters

    2 Brigade: 6-pdr foot battery: Hauptmann Goschl

2nd Army Division.

Artillery commander Major Colonge, Major Josef Halder.

    1 Brigade: 6-pdr light battery: Hauptmann von Caspers

    2nd Brigade: 6-pdr light battery: Hauptmann von Tonne.

    1 Brigade: 12-pdr foot battery; Hauptmann Torn.

    2 Brigade 6-pdr foot battery: Hauptmann Binder

Reserve Artillery.

    Kombinierte fahrende battery: Hauptmann Koppelt

    6-pdr foot battery: Hauptmann Strissl

    12-pdr foot battery: Hauptmann Taush.

    Parc: Hauptmann Brad.

In 1806. Bavaria fielded two light 6-pdr batterys, 4x 6-pdr foot batteries, 2x 12-pdr batteries, and a kombinierte battery, which consisted of 4x 12-pdr, 2x 7-pdr howitzers and 2x 6-pdrs, of which all the guns were of Austrian design bar two 12-pdrs.. The 12-pdr batteries acted as position batteries.

In 1807, Napoleon elevated Maximilian Joseph to King Maximilian I of Bavaria who gained the Free Cities of Augsburg and Nuremberg but lost Julich and Berg to form the Grand Duchy of Berg for Marshal Joachim Murat. On 10th January 1807, Württemberg and Bavrian troops formed IX of the Grande Armee, the artillery organisation was as follows [28]:

1st Division.
Artillery commander: Major Graf von Spreti
Kombinietre battery: Hauptmann Koppelt, assisted by Hauptmann Regnier
    6-pdr foot battery: Hauptmann Goschl
    6-pdr foot battery: Hauptmann von Hofftetten
    12-pdr foot battery: Hauptmann Peters.

Reserve-Parc: Major Josef Halder
    6-pdr foot battery: hauptmann Strissl

2nd Division.
Artillery commander: Lt-Colonel Baron de Colonge.
    6-pdr light battery: Hauptmann von Caspers
    6-pdr light battery: Hauptmann von Tonne
    6-pdr foot battery: Hauptmann Graf von Leiningen
    6-pdr foot battery: Hauptmann Tausch

---
28 Lutz 1894 p44

Reserve-Parc: Major Colonge

12-pdr foot battery: Hauptmann Brad.

As well, a 6-pdr foot battery was stationed in the Tirol, Battery Torn was in the corps of French Marshall Brune in Prussia.

On 24th December 1807 four artillery commands were created, the first in Munchen, the second in Augsburg, the third in Bamberg and the fourth at Innsbrud.

In 1809, fought against the Austrians as VIII Corps in Germany and the Tyrol. In 1809, thirteen artillery companies served in VII (Bavarian) Corps and 1 artillery company in the Tyrol. The artillery having been divided into three divisions for the campaign under the order of 26th February 1809, being 1x wurst battery of 6 guns, 2x foot batteries of 6 guns each , and 1x 12-pdr battery of 6 guns. The Artillery Directory assumed direct control of the ouvrier company and added an additional NCO and 6 gunstock makers. On 3rd May 1809, the King agreed to the arming of the gunners with muskets. Previously, as in the Prussian army, it had been considered presumptuous for artillery men to carry muskets, except for immediate self defence or doing sentry duty in emergency's. Each company was initially issued 25 muskets, later increased to 50.

Bavarian foot artillery battery in action in 1809. (S H Smith).

The organisation of the artillery mobilised for the 1809 campaign was as follows [29]:

Commander of Mobilised artillery: Baron de Colonge.

1 Division.

Artillery commander: Major Josef Halder

    6-pdr light battery: Hauptmann Regnier

    6-pdr foot battery: Hauptmann Wagner

    6-pdr foot battery: Hauptmann von Tonne

    12-pdr reserve foot battery: Hauptmann von Hofftetten

2 Division.

Artillery commander: Major Baron Zoller

    6-pdr light battery: Hauptmann von Caspers

    6-pdr foot battery: Hauptmann Torn

---

[29] Lutz 1894 47

6-pdr foot battery: Hauptmann Ullmer

12-pdr reserve battery: Hauptmann von Berchen

3 Division.

Artillery commander: Major Lamen

6-pdr light battery: Hauptmann Gotthard

6-pdr foot battery: Hauptmann Bamler

6-pdr foot battery: Hauptmann Rons

12-pdr reserve battery: Hauptmann Dietrich

On 29th April 1811, the "Koniglichtes Artillerie-Corps" (Royal Artillery Corps) formed from the light (horse) artillery, foot artillery and artillery train.

In 1812, Bavaria sent ten batteries into Russia and formed the 19th and 20th Division of VI (Bavarian) Corps (30x 6-pdrs, 8x 12-pdrs and 20x Howitzers).[30]

19th (Bavarian) Division (Oberst Freiherr von Lamney)

1st Light Battery (OberstLt. Carl Freiherr von Widemann) [3 6-pdr, 1 Howitzer]

3rd Light Battery (Captain Georg Halder III) [3 6-pdr, 1 Howitzer]

1st Foot (6-pdr) Battery (Captain Baptist von Brack) [6 6-pdr, 2 howitzers]

---

30 Lutz 1894

      6th Foot (12-pdr) Battery (Captain Bartholomaus Rois) [4 12-pdr, 2 howitzers]

      Howitzer Battery [6 Howitzers]

20th (Bavarian) Division (OberstLt von Zoller)

      2nd Light Battery (Captain Joseph Gotthard) [3 6-pdr, 1 Howitzer]

      4th Light Battery (Captain Carl L. Baron von Gravenreuth) [3 6-pdr, 1 Howitzer]

      4th Line (12-pdr) Battery (Captain Maximilian Berchem) [4 12-pdr, 2 howitzers]

      5th Line (6-pdr) Battery (Captain Franz von Hofstetten) [6 6-pdr, 2 howitzers]

      8th Line (6-pdr) Battery (Captain Peter Ulmer) [6 6-pdr, 2 howitzers]

12-pdr Battery (124 men, 64 horse) of 1812

      4 12-pdr, 2 howitzers, 10 12-pdr Caissons, 4 Howitzer Caissons, 1 Field Forge, 1 Coal Wagon and 1 Supply Wagon.

6-pdr Battery (112 men, 68 horses) of 1812

      6 6-pdr, 2 howitzers, 14 6-pdr Caissons, 4 Howitzer Caissons, 1 Infantry Munition Wagon, 1 Field Forge, 1 Coal Wagon, 1 Supply Wagon.

The rescript of March 6 1813 reformed the artillery regiment with twenty one companies, primarily manned by gunners who had been discharged from the service before 1812. The transport battalion was also reformed, but due to lack of equipment, men and horses, it was rebuilt one division at a time. By 1813 the Bavarian army had six 6-pdr batteries (two per division) and four 12-pdr batteries forming the artillery reserve. The organisation of the artillery on 6 March 1813 was as follows [31]:

Commander of Mobilised Artillery: Major General Baron Colonge

1 Division.
Artillery commander: Lt-Colonel: Goschl
    6-pdr light battery: Hauptmann Rudersheim
    6-pdr foot battery: Hauptmann Fintenaur

2 Division.
Artillery commander: Lt-Colonel von Caspers
    6-pdr light battery: Hauptmann Aign
    6-pdr foot battery: Hauptmann Danner

3 Division.
Artillery commander: Major Wagner
    6-pdr light battery: Hauptmann Halder

---
31 Lutz 1894 p59

6-pdr foot battery: Hauptmann Achner

Reserve.

Commander: Major Marabini

    6-pdr light battery: Hauptman Baron Widnmann

    12-pdr foot battery: Hauptmann Weissner

    12-pdr foot battery: Hauptmann: Ulmer

    12-pdr foot battery: Hauptmann Dietrich

    12-pdr foot battery: Hauptmann Bamler.

On March 27th 1813, the artillery establishment was as follows:

Wurst Artillery: 4x officers, 12x NCO's, 2x trumpeters, 1x smith, 4x train NCO's, 1x Train trumpeter, 2x 7-pdr howitzer, 6x 6-pdrs, 8x wurst wagons, 9x munition wagons, 1x field forge, 1xcoal wagon, 1xsupply wagon.

The organisation of a 6-pdr Foot Battery was : 4x officers, 4x train NCO's, 2x 7-pdr howitzer, 6x 6-pdr 14x caissons, 1x infantry caisson, 1x field forge, 1 xcoal wagon, 1x supply wagon.

For a heavy foot battery of 12-pdr field guns, the organisation was: 4x officers, 4x train NCO's, 2x 7-pdr, 6x 12-pdr, 20x caissons, 1x field forge, 1x coal wagon, 1x supply wagon.

Bavarian 1785 wurst wagon. (S H Smith).

At this time the field artillery consisted of four 6-pdr batteries, four 12-pdr batteries and four wurst or light artillery batteries. The Wurst Wagons were those designed in 1800 by Manson, replacing those of 1785. The Wurst and 6-pdr batteries had 112 men each and the 12-pdr batteries 124 men each. In addition there was an artillery reserve with two 12-pdr foot batteries and a battery of six 10-pdr howitzers. The transport battalion also formed a pontoon train of 1,078 men and 633 draft horses, the organisation being 1 field bridge inspector, 1x 1st Lieutenant, 1x 2nd Lieutenant, 6x corporals, 1x fourier, 2x drummers, 28x 1st pontononiers, 58x pontooniers. The force was charged with manning the water, road and bridge building services of the army. The company was raised in Braunau on the River Inn under the orders of General Wrede and outfitted with 25 Austrian Pontoons carried on haquet wagons converted from farm lurries. The corps was finally active on 17th October 1813, and its organisation remained unchanged until 1822.

A siege park was also formed, commanded by the Artillery Directory, and consisted of 4x 24-pdr, 8x 18-pdr, 12x 12-pdr, 4x 10-pdr howitzers, 4x 7-pdr howitzers, 4x 60-pdr mortars, and 4x 30-pdr mortars. The Bavarian artillery remained at this organisation until 26th June 1816.

With the Allies.

On 12th October 1813, sensing that the tide of war had turned, Maximilian gradually shifted to the side of the Allies in as dignified a fashion as he could manage. Formed 5th Corps of the Army of Bohemia. In 1814, Bavaria handed back the Tyrol to Austria.

In 1815, General Wrede invaded France with his 4th (Bavarian) Corps: Exchanged Salzburg with Austria in return for Wurzburg and much of Frankfurt am Main. The organisation of the artillery in 4th Corps was as follows [32]:

Field Artillery Commander: Lieutenant General Baron Colonge

1 Division.

Artillery commander: Lieutenant Colonel von Caspers.
    6-pdr battery: Hauptmann Danner
    12-pdr battery: Hauptmann Denrer

2 Division.

Artillery commander: Major Wagner
    6-pdr battery: Hauptmann Weisshaupt
    12-pdr battery: Hauptmann Berueff

3 Division.

Artillery Commander: Major Von Hofftetten
    6-pdr battery: Hauptmann Achner
    12-pdr battery: Hauptmann Ulmer

4 Division.

Artillery commander: Major von Gotthard
    6-pdr battery: Hauptmann van La Rojee

---

32 Lutz 1894 p63

12-pdr battery: Hauptmann: Weisshaupt

1 Cavalry Division.
    6-pdr light battery: Hauptmann Rudershelim
    6-pdr light battery: Hauptmann von Halder
    12-pdr reserve battery: Hauptmann Ott

Artillery Reserve.
Commander: Lieutenant-Colonel Marabini
    6-pdr light battery: Hauptmann Baron Widnmann
    6-pdr light battery: Hauptmann Aign
    12-pdr battery: Hauptmann Rathgeber
    10-pdr howitzer battery: Hauptmann Baron Gumppenberg

On 26th June 1816, the artillery regiment was expanded to four battalions of six companies.[33]

---

33 Nafziger GF (1993), *The Armies of the Kingdom of Bavaria and the Grand Duchy of Würzburg 1792-1815,* Nafziger Collection.

Bavarian Horse Artillery.

In August 1799, an experimental Horse Artillery Company was founded Captain von Schweinichen who as served as a Lieutenant in the Prussian Horse Artillery. Special 6-pdr canons were constructed. At Hohenlinden (3rd December 1800), this Horse Artillery Company (6 6-pdr and 2 howitzers) got stuck on a road and was taken prisoner by the French. On 14th May 1801, the reconstituted Horse Artillery company was made by the elector independent of the Artillery Regiment.

Horse Battery of 7th April 1802 (113 Mounts, 64 Draft Horses, 24 Pack Horses):

> 6 6-pdr cannon, 2 7-pdr cannon, 1 Captain, 1 Oberleutnant, 2 Unterleutnant, 2 Oberfeuerwerkers, 1 Furier, 1 Wachmeister, 1 Company Surgeon, 2 Feuerwerkers, 6 Corporals, 3 Trumpeters, 6 Bombardier 1st Class, 6 Bombadier 2nd Class, 18 Gunners 1st Class, 54 Gunners 2nd Class, 10 Gunners 2nd Class (dismounted), 1 Leatherworker, 1 Farrier, 1 Saddlemaker, 1 Cartwright, 2 Foremen, 48 Labourers, 12 Reserve Labourers, 113 Mounts,

The battery was commanded by Captain von Schweinechen.

On 14th March 1804, the horse company was disbanded with its personnel distributed among the foot artillery companies of the Artillery Regiment. With the disbanding the battery the following officers retired from the service:

Major Schweinichen, Captain, Tausch, Oberleutnent von Caspers, and Unterleutnents von Willenfels and Rohr.

The Regimental History of the 1st Field Artillery Regiment "Prinz-Regent Luitpold", Volume 2 (1806-1824) stated that light batteries were introduced after the experiments made during the 1806-7 war with Austrian "Wurst" Wagons. On 20th October 1808, the King off Bavaria decided to introduce one "light battery" per artillery battalion. These light batteries were provided with 6-pdr guns of the regular foot artillery and "Wurst" Wagons for the transportation and ammunition (6-pdr Wurst carried 70 roundshot and 10 canister shots).

The Riding (Horse) Company of 1812

> 1x Oberfeuerwerker, 1x Fourier, 2 xCorporal-Feuerwerker, 6x Corporals, 12x Bombardier, 18x Gunner 1st Class, 50x Gunner 2nd Class, 1x Trumpet and 1x Praktikant.

Horse Battery of 1812 (112 men, 64 draft horses and 24 pack horses)

> 3x 6-pdr, 1x 7-pdr howitzers, 4x 6-pdr Wurst Wagons, 2x Howitzer Wurst Wagons, 5x Munition Wagons, 1x Cavalry Munition Wagon, 1x Field Forge, 1x Coal Wagon, 1x Supply Wagon.

Field Artillery Equipment.

By 1800. Bavaria had about 80 guns many of which were Rumford designs, In 1805, Bavaria deployed four batteries being deployed against Austria. In 1809, Bavaria had 72 guns in service with Grande Armee and all the 60 guns sent to Russia in 1812 were lost.

From 1785 Austrian 3-pdr, 6-pdr and 12-pdr guns with a 7-pdr howitzer were used in Bavaria replacing the Valliere style guns. A wurst wagon was used by the light artillery.

Bavarian 1785 wurst caisson. (S H Smith).

Rumford System M1791.

In 1791, Rumford introduced his own 3-pdr, 6-pdr and 7-pdr howitzer which served as battalion artillery. Rumford's new carriage designs were based on his observation of British Artillery whilst in England as Under Secretary of State, and his service with the British Army in America in 1784-5 as Colonel of his own Dragoon Regiment. Rumford took the concept of the Desagulier's block trail, and modified the system for his 3-pdr.

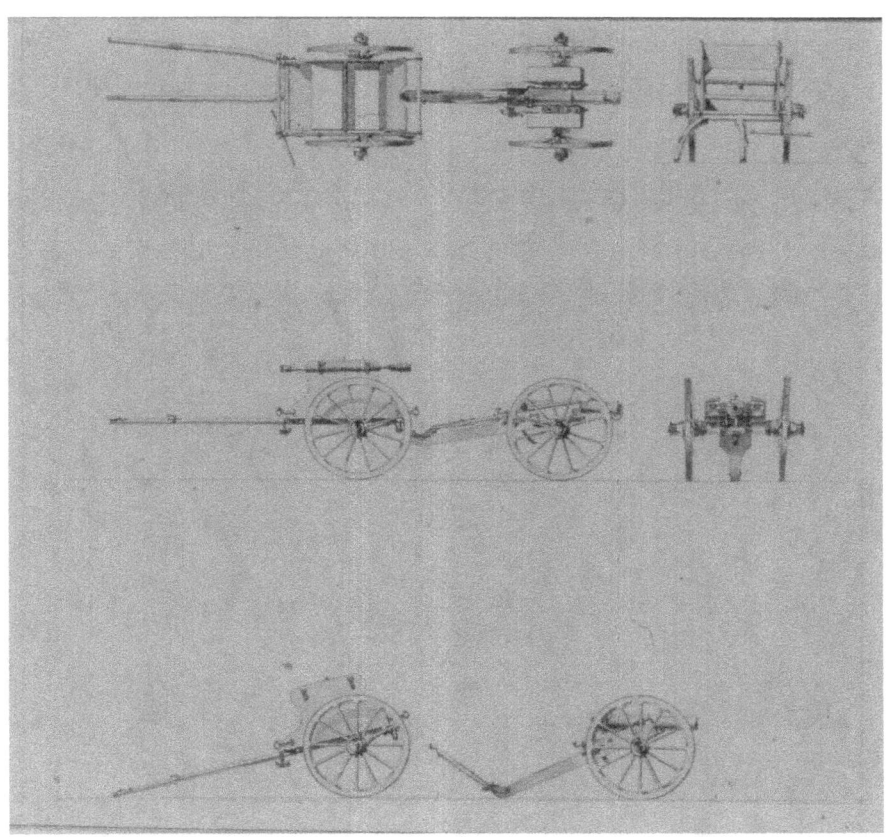
Rumford light 3-pdr. This design was based on then current English designs. (S H Smith).

He abandoned limbers, and instead for the light guns (3-pdr and 6-pdr) which he replaced with an ammunition limber which could carry 4 or 6 gunners. Each gun had two limbers and so could carry up to 12 gunners. There was no differentiation it seems between light artillery or horse artillery. Rumford also devised a new howitzer which had a maximum elevation of 86-degrees, and could be fired whilst still attached to the limber. Rumford also designed heavy siege guns, mortars as well as a 12-pdr field gun and 7-pdr howitzer for use with the field artillery. Both the 7-pdr howitzer and 6-pdr field gun shared a common bracket carriage design, the light 3-pdr being mounted on a block trail.

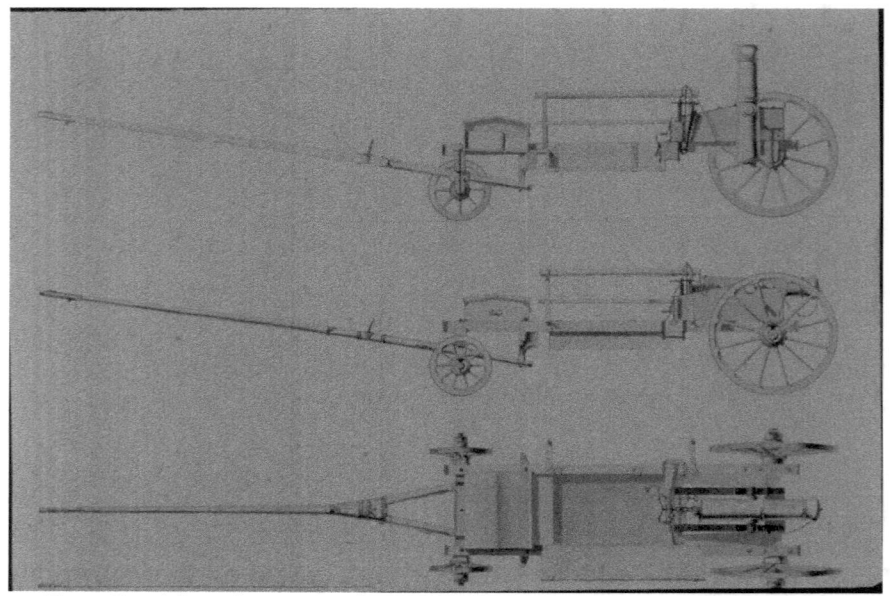

Rumford howizter carriage, able to fire at high angle. (S H Smith).

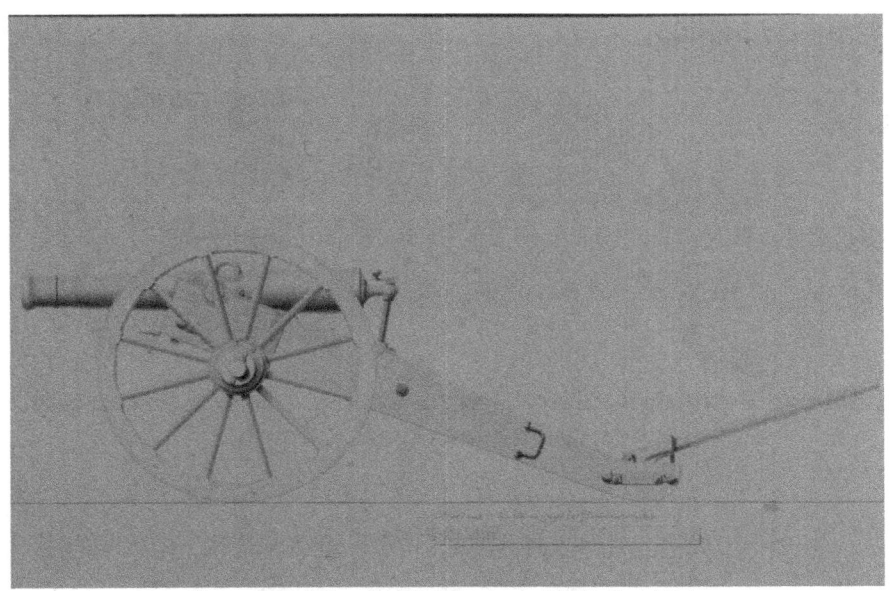

Rumford 6-pdr field gun. (S H Smith).

Pfalz Artillery Schweinchen M1799.

The Pfalz artillery consisted of one company of gunners, armed with French Valliere guns. GL von Schweinichen was brought into the service by Elector Max Joseph earlier in the year of 1799. On 30 August 1799, with the intention of improving the artillery of the Pfalz, he instigated the casting of 6-pdr guns, with a total length of 16 calibres based on patterns provided by Berlin for the horse artillery. The Pfalz guns were lost at Hohenlinden. With the union of Bavaria and the Pfalz in 1799/1800, the artillery came under the direction of Jakob Manson in Munich.

Manson M1801.

Mansin 6-pdr gun tubes. Their design was based on the gun tubes of Gribeauval. (S H Smith).

In the summer of 1800, Manson led a group that was charged with designing a new system of artillery for the unified Bavaria, The Rumford 3-pdr, 6-pdr and howitzer were retained, along with the 7-pdr howitzer. New limbers were introduced on the Austrian system. Also introduced were new 6-pdr and 12-pdr, which retained the calibres used by Rumford, and were an amalgam of Gribeauval and AnXI French gun tube and carriage designs. The total length of the tube was 18calibres. Carriages were those designed by Manson and used the elevating screw and plate of the Gribeauval system rather than the vertical screw acting on the back-weight of the gun tube of Rumford designs. A new Wurst wagon was introduced to replace the M1785 wagon. In 1805 Rumford returned to Bavaria as director of Artillery.

Manson 7-pdr howitzer gun tube. (S H Smith).

A total of 76 guns of this type cast by 1806.

Two types of caisson were in use the reserve caisson to Gribeauval designs for use with the heavy and foot batteries and wurst caisson for the light artillery.

Loading for the reserve caissons was as follows:

6-pdr Caisson (one caisson per gun): 115 cartridges and ball were carried, 25 canister, along with 50 balls and their powder bags, 200 priming tubes 25 quick matches and 12 toises of slow match.

- Partition 1: 6 bricoles, 2 charge bags, the rest of the contents being as for a 12-pdr.
- Partitions 2 and 6: 6 cartridges and ball.
- Partitions 3 and 5: 6 cartridges and ball

- Partitions 7 and 8: 8 cartridges and ball
- Partition 9: 8 cartridges and ball
- Partitions 10 to 17 and 21: same as Partition 7 and 8
- Partitions 18 to 20: same as Partition 9.

Caisson for a 12-pdr (two caisson per 12-pdr gun). 48 cartridges and ball were carried, 20 balls, 22 powders balls, 100 priming tubes, 11 quick matches, 12 toises of slow match. Caisson 1 also carried 10 bricoles.
- Partition 1: 3 sacs a charge, 1 fuse pouch, one linstock, three hand spikes, two porte-lance, two finger stalls, two spatulas for making the fuses with.
- Partitions 2 + 3: 4 cartridges and ball and two bags of powder in each.
- Partition 4: 6 bags of powder.
- Partition 5 and 16: 4 cartridges and ball
- Partition 17: same as partition 4
- Partition 18 and 20: same as 2 and 3

7-pdr Howitzer Caisson (one caisson per light howitzer, two per heavy howitzer) In total 42 bombs and their powder charges were carried along with 6 cannister

- Partition 1: 2 hand spikes, two quick matched, two fingerstalls, two powder measures, four fuse chasers, two mallets.
- Partition 2 and 3: 25 powder bags.
- Partition 4: 3 powder bags and balls, 70 fuses, 9 quick matches, two pairs of bombardier's cuffs, 12 toises (24-m) of slow match.
- Partition 5: 10 bricoles.

Loading for the wurst caissons was as follows:

6-pdr (one caisson per gun). On caisson limber 40 round shot and 10 cannister, in caisson, 50 round shot and 10 cannister.

7-pdr light howitzer: on limber 18 shells and 6 cannister, in the caisson, 24 shells and 6 cannister,

Each battery also had a tool wagon that carried tools for general repairs. All the tools needed to carry out field repairs were carried in one of the caissons of the battery, which in action was kept at the rear with all the other spare wagons. Smaller tools were kept in a series of wooden boxes inside the caisson along with the other spare items and larger tools.

The 1800 Wurst Wagon based on contemporary prints could carry 12 gunners, and appears to have been an improved version of the 1785 equipment. Like the caisson it too carried a forage rack on its rear. By 1812 limbers for the light artillery, and foot artillery could carry three drivers mounted on the ammunition box. These limbers replaced both the Rumford designs of 1791 and Manson's 1801 design which was copied by the French in 1803. Rumfords design was based on the British 1788 Desaguliers system, and Mansons on the 1774 limber design of Austria. This new limber design was universal to all guns and rolling stock.

Austrian Wurst Horse Artillery 1806.

As a reward for the support of Bavaria during the 1805 campaign, during the occupation of Vienna, Napoleon presented the Elector Max Joseph with two batteries of Austrian 6-pdr cavalry artillery guns and support vehicles, which were used to mobilize two more batteries [16 Austrian Cavalerie Artillerie guns added. 6-pdr (x12) 7-pdr Howizter (x4). In 1806, Lieutenant-General of Artillery Jakob Manson, removed the Wurst seats from the guns, the gunners riding on the M1800 wurst wagon.

Napoleon also presented the Bavarian artillery with cannon boring machines and other equipment used in the manufacture of cannon from the Vienna arsenal, which were set up in Munich and Amberg. With this machine, once the gun tubes had been cast, the tubes were bored in a two stage process. The first stage was carried out at the place of casting, Munich and finished at Amberg. The basic shape of the tube was making a mould either in lime or sand. Six men could cast a 12lb from raw metal in five hours. The cold tube was placed on a giant water powder lathe (invented by Maritz) where it was rotated around a static cutting head to cut the bore of the tube. The outside of the tub was also finished on a lathe to remove any imperfections. Once the bore was finished, the vent was drilled out. Initially this was a narrow diameter bore cut from the outside of the tube to the bore at an angle of some 7 degrees. . The machine was driven by water power, like that of furance, with a force of 6-8 horsepower, which turned the wheels 16times a minute. The trunnions were then finished after the vent had been drilled. The bore was then drilled to the full width. A 3-pdr required 20hours of boring, a 6-pdr 24 hours, a 7-pdr howitzer 22 hours and 12pdr 25 hours to complete the process.

A paid gun founder was appointed. Gun production was handled by the Ouvrier company, which had four squads, one of wheel-wrights, one of canon borers, one of smiths, and one of carpenters, which was commanded day by day by Colonel

Lintz, and from 21st June 1807 was directly commanded by the Director of the Arsenals. With this equipment cannon production could be increased, the gun tubes being the same calibre as Austria.

With Manson's death on 5th January 1809, directorship of the arsenal was taken over by Colonel Comeau and Captain von Reichenbach. New Wurst wagons were introduced by 1812. Organisation of a Bavarian 6-pdr Battery in 1809 was 4x 6-pdr and 2x 7-pdr Howitzer. In 1812 the equipment organisation was a follows:

Bavarian 6-pdr Battery of 1812 (112 men, 68 horses) 6x 6-pdr, 2 x7-pdr howitzers, 14x 6-pdr Caissons, 4 Howitzer Caissons, 1x Infantry Munition Wagon, 1x Field Forge, 1x Coal Wagon, 1x Supply Wagon.

Bavarian 12-pdr Battery (124 men, 64 horse) of 1812 had 4x 12-pdr, 2x howitzers, 10x 12-pdr Caissons, 4x Howitzer Caissons, 1x Field Forge, 1 xCoal Wagon and 1x Supply Wagon.

Bavarian Horse Artillery Company had 4x 6-pdr, 2x 7-pdr howitzers, 4x 6-pdr Wurst Wagons, 2x

Howitzer Wurst Wagons, 5x Munition Wagons, 1x Cavalry Munition Wagon, 1x Field Forge, 1x Coal Wagon, 1x Supply Wagon.

French Guns M1808.

Most of the Kingdoms artillery material was lost in 1812, and the field artillery had to be rebuilt around surviving guns. By March 1813, 120 field guns and 436 caissons were in service of the French pattern. A report of the 1st August 1813 lists the Bavarian artillery having 10 foot batteries armed with 6x 6-pdr and 2x 5.72-inch howitzers, 4 light (Wurst) batteries armed with 4x 6-pdr (in theory 6x 6-pdr according to Rescript of March 1813 which does not seem to have been acted upon due to shortages of equipment and French guns had been used in the place of Bavarian Manson M1800) and two 5.72inch howitzers, and 2 reserve batteries armed with 6x 12-pdr and two 6.32inch howitzers.

These French guns were of the M1808 system. Artillery in France had undergone major changes since 1803, which were not the benefit of the artillery.

With the defection of General von Wrede in 1813, the Bavarian artillery was hampered by the lack of ammunition as the French guns were of a different calibre to those of the allies. Non French ammunition could be fired, but with greater windage, reducing the effectivness of the guns. This was a major contributing factor to the defeat of Wrede at Hanau. French guns were used after the decree of December 1806 which made the French calibre standard throughout the French Empire, and of vassal states serving with the Grande Armee. French guns were probably also used until sufficient Bavarian equipment could be produced.

Siege Artillery Equipment.

A siege train was re-established in October 1813. The bronze guns included long 6-pdr, 12-pdr, 24-pdr and the short French AnXI 24-pdr. Long and short 10 and 25 livre howitzers, 10, 25, and 60 livre mortars. In Iron, were 6-pdrs, 12-pdrs, 18-pdrs a 60 livre pierrier and a 12-livre coehorn mortar. The gun carriages and support vehicles were all to Gribeauval system design.

The Gribeauval system of siege artillery as devised in 1765, and based on the 1732 artillery system of Lavalliere in France was based on 8-pdr, 12-pdr, 16-pdr and 24-pdr guns supported by an 8inch (223mm)howitzer.

Gribeauval's sieges guns, relying on designs of 1732 were less obviously superior to the system that they replaced, when compared to the modifcation's to the garrison and field artillery, and performed little better than their predecessors. Few of these guns were produced until further tests were carried out in 1786, but the guns performance was very unsatisfactory, the gun tubes lasting some 100rounds.

The gun carriages were similar to those of 1732, retained the wooden axle, but the wooden wedge for aiming the piece was replaced with a boring machine of Austrian inspired designs. The siege train was a lot slower to move than the field artillery, the heavier ammunition being carried in special carts rather than caissons. On campaign the gun carriages were moved seperatly to the gun tubes, which were carried on a sling cart, both vehicles being drawn by four horses each..

A mountain artillery company was raised armed with 3-pdr guns and a short 7-livre howitzer.

IBavarian light artillery gunners mounted on the wurst wagon. (S H Smith).

Ordnance Innovators: Bavaria

Graf von Rumford (Sir Benjamin Thompson) (1753-1814)
Born in Massachusetts in 1753. Fellow of the Royal Society (1779). Between 1777-1784, Under Secretary of State in Lord North's Administration (Britain). In 1783 Benjamin Thompson was brought into Bavarian service by the elector. In the following decade the Bavarian army was reformed mainly due to his influence, who although mainly a chemist (and inventor of the coffee percolator and who wrote an important treatise on gunpowder based on his experiments in England between 1776 and 1783) altered their uniform and introduced a new ordnance.

Between 1784-85, he returned to north America at the fall of North's ministry as Colonel of his own Dragoon Regiment where he saw the Desegulier Block Trail in action. In 1785, joined Bavaria Civil and Military service, serving as Minister of War and Police and Grand Chamberlain. In 1791, he received a British Knighthood. In 1792, made Graf von Rumford of the Holy Roman Empire (after the place where he was born near Concord, New Hampshire).

In Bavaria, he designed the Rumford System of Artillery and reformed Bavarian gun powder production. His interest in field artillery led him to study the boring and firing of cannons, his artillery designs were so highly regarded that by 1799 US President Adams tried to persuade him to return to America to found a Military Academy.

Co-founder of the Royal Institution in 1800. In 1802, moved to Paris and married the widow of the chemist Lavoisier.

In 1805, recalled to Munich when French and Austrian forces threatened it and chaired the Artillery Committee. Was Refused as Bavarian Ambassador to England as he was a British Citizen. August 1814 Died of 'nervous fever' in Auteuil. Furthered the careers of General Wrede and Humphrey Davy whom he appointed as lecturer in chemistry to the Royal Institution.

Schweinichen, Georg Alexander (1752-1832)

Born 3 February 1752 in Berlin. On 4 November 1768, 2nd Lt in the Prussian artillery and in 1779 left due to illness. On 24 September 1790, Major in United Belgian State Artillery. On 22 March 1793, 1st Lt in 2nd Dutch Artillery Brigade, 8.August 1799, Pfalz Artillery Hauptmann and built the Pfalz horse artillery battery; 25 April 1801 major; 14 March 1804 pensioned; 28 March 1809 Oberst-Lt and Pfatz- commandant. Died 5.March 1832 in Bamberg.

Manson System

In 1800, Jakob Manson was made GL and Director of Artillery and director who along, Baron Zoller, Sebastian Joseph de Comeau de Cherry and Baron Colonges and Lintz, a carpenter from Alsace, who had served with Manson in the army of the Conde was placed in charge of the artillery workers assigned to making new carriages. It was under Manson's leadership that a War

Commissioner who was responsible for the delivery and consumption of military munitions and ancillary equipment, and for the purchase of all artillery equipment was appointed. He was also responsible for the metals used in the cannon foundry and salt petre production.[34]

Manson Jacques Charles (Jakob) (1724-1809).

Born in Provence in 1725 and joined the French Artillery in 1742 as a cadet, graduating as an officer in 1745. He worked alongside Gribeauval et al in reforming the French artillery after the experiences of the Seven Years War and wrote several ballistics papers. Served in America.

On 9 March 1788, he was made Marshall. In 1792, along with Comte Rostaign he revised the Gribeauval system and published the resulting treatise detailing changes to French artillery between 1764 and 1791.

In 1792 Manson France to serve in the Army of the Condee. In 1797, joined the Russian Army, and was promoted to General. In 1799, joined the Bavarian service. On 6 February made Lt-General of Artillery and on 1 October 1801 founded the artillery school. From 1800-to his death in 1809 he was the Zeughaus director

---

[34] Nafziger GF (1993), The Armies of the Kingdom of Bavaria and the Grande Duchy of Wurzburg 1792-1815, Nafziger Collection.

designing the Artillery rollingstock. Saw service in the military campaigns of 1742-1748, 1793-1800. Died in Munich in 1809.[35]

Colonge 1754-1837

French Émigré officer, fought with the Royalist Army of the Conde, entered Bavarian service in 1800 and worked alongside Jakob Manson. In 1822, General Director of Bavarian Artillery.

Lintz

A carpenter from Alsace, who had served with Manson in the army of the Conde and placed in charge of the artillery workers assigned to making new carriages.

Karl Julien Zoller (1773-1849)

Gentleman cadet of artillery in Anhalt, by 1792 he had entered the French service, and in 1795 he joined the Royalist Army of the Conde. Entered Bavarian service in 1799 and worked alongside Manson with rank of Colonel. 1818 made a military commissioner, Major-General 1824, introduced a new artillery system in 1836, made GL and Commander of Artillery of Bavaria

---

[35] Xylander, R. Ritter v. (1905), *Geschichte des 1. Feld-Artillerie-Regiments Prinz-Regent Luitpold.* Vol. I, E. S. Mittler, Berlin

Chapter 6: Hesse-Darmstadt

A state with a long history of world wide, efficient military service, Hesse-Darmstadt was an original member of the Confederation, with a contingent of 4,000 men. Its troops served in all the French Empire's wars well into 1813, and attained a high reputation for courage and fidelity.

In 1752, the Hessian Artillery was formed to man regimental artillery pieces, and only on 7th April 1790 was it formed into a Field Artillery Regiment on under the command of Major Johann Fischer. The calibres used were 3-pdr, 6-pdr, 12-pdr field guns and 7-pdr and 10-pdr howitzers, cast in bronze to the Gribeauval style and mounted on Gribeauval carriages. In 1792, Captain Georg Gottleib Hahn succeeded him and remained as commander certainly until 1814 with some sources saying he remained in post till his death in 1823. By 1800, a new system of artillery had been brought into service, the 12-pdr being taken out of service and placed in the siege train along with the 4-pdr and a new and lighter 6-pdr introduced. The guns were inspired by the French system and were cast at Marxburg under the supervision of Colonel Hahn (1756-1823), who oversaw all construction of field guns and attendant rolling stock. It was he who introduced the Gribeauval designed caisson, as well as Prussian 7-pdr and 10-pdr howitzers.

The Hessian field artillery corps was formed on 7th April 1790, out of the existing artillery company's, the first company being raised at this time, the second company following on 30th April, the organisation of 1st company being as follows:

1 Lieutenant Colonel (Oberstluetnent), 1 Captain, 1 1st Lieutenant, 1 Pyrotechnician, 1 sergent-major, 1 sergent, 6 corporals, 1 drummer, 1 Zeugwart, 60 gunners

The 2nd company had 72 men, and the first 75. The artillery establishment was re-organised in Septmeber 1790 to:

1st Company: 1 Captain, 1st Lieutenant, 2 2nd Lieutenant, 10 NCO, 1 surgeon, 1 drummer, 67 gunners, 2 staff officers.
2nd Company: 1 captain, 2 2nd lieutenant, 10 NCO, 1 drummer, 65 gunners.

A battalion artillery company was also organised in September 1790 for the Fusilier battalion and consisted of two 3-pdr guns. This organisation remained in effect until

September 1793, when the corps was significantly re-organised on the following lines:[36]

1st Company: 1 Major, 2 Staff Captains, 5 Subalterns, 1 surgeon, 14 NCO, 1Drummer, 120 gunners, 70 handlanger, 135 horses.
2nd Company: 1 captain, 3 subalterns, 1 suregon, 14 NCO, 1 drummer, 119 gunners, 60 handlanger, 126 horses.
Middle and Lower Staff: 2 Zeugwart, 1 clerk, 1 saddlemaker, 1 wagon maker, 2 smiths, 1 wagonmaster, 2 wheel-wrights, 3 horses.

This gave the corps a total of 422 men and 264 horses. The guns were of French inspired designs of 3-pdr, 6-pdr and 12-pdr calibres. The woodwork at the time was light blue.

The order of 26th November and that of 12th December 1795 raised artillery companies for each of the infantry regiments, to act as regimental or battalion artillery, being equipped and organised as follows:

1st Battalion Leib Regiment:

---

[36] Schafer and Wagner <u>Das Landgraflich hessich Artilleriekorps: Uniformierung der hessen-darmstadtischen Artillery 1790-1803</u> In *Depesche Magazine* N. 27

1 officer, 3 NCO, 24 gunners, 13 handlngaer, 29 horses, 2 6-pdr, 2 munition wagons, 1 infantry wagon, 1 baggage wagon, 180 round shot, 68 canister rounds, 1790 musket flints.

2nd Battalion Leib Regiment:
1 officer, 36 NCO, 24 gunners, 11 handlanger, 21 horses, 2 6-pdr, 2 munition wagons, 1 infantry wagon, 1 baggage wagon. 180 round shot, 68 canister rounds, 1820 musket flints.

2nd Grenadier Battalion:
1 Occier, 3 NCO, 24 gunners, 11 handlnager, 21 horses, 2 6-pdr, 2 munition wagons, 1 baggage wagon, 180 round shot, 68 canister rounds, 688 musket flints.

Artillery Reserve:
8 NCO, 38 gunners, 10 handlnager, 3 musicians, 6 baggage wagons.

For the 1806 campaign, Hesse-Darmstadt did not field its entire artillery force. A single company was fielded which ocnistsed of 137 men organised as follows:

1 captain, 1 1st Lieutenant, 1 2nd Lieutenant, 1 senior pyrotechnician, 1 pyrotechnician, 1 Feldwebel, 2 sergents, 8 corporals, 2 drummers, 3 bombardiers, 7 first gunners.

The train detachment consisted of 1 wagon master, 4 corporals, 80 handlanger, 3 officers batmen, 1 saddlemaker, 1 blacksmith, 1 wheelwright, 1 blacksmiths assistant.

Based on French archival sources, the artillery was re-organised in November 1806 for the Winter Campaign, the new organisation being:

1 captain, 1 l1st lieutenant, 2 2nd lieutenants, 1 feldwebel, 2 sergents. 4 corporapls, 2 drummers, 14 bombardiers, 74 gunners, 1 surgeon, 1 vetinarian, 1 baggage master, 1 driver-artisan, 1 blacksmith, 1wheel-wright, 1 master driver, 4-6pdr guns, 2 6.32inch howitzers, 2 replacement carriages, 18 caissons and 6 forges.

This organisation and equipment appears to have remained the same until a further re-organisation took place in December 1807, when the artillery division assigned to the infantry brigades was increased from eight to ten guns, consisting of 2 7-pdr howitzers and 8 6-pdr, being manned by

1 NCO, 2 first gunners and 10 gunners. Every pair of guns was commanded by a lieutenant, a captain commanding the division, the organisation of the 174 assigned men being as follows:

1 staff officer, 1 captain, 1 1st lieutenant, 2 2nd lieutenants, 1 senior pyrotechnician, 2 pyrotechnicians, 2 feldwebel, 6 sergeants, 6 corporals, 1 surgeon, 9 bombardiers, 16 first gunners, 125 cannoneersm, 2 musicians

The staff of the artillery as a whole consisted of one colonel, one staff officer, one adjutant, one surgeon and his assistant, one clerk, one oberzeugwart, one unterzeugwart, When the Duchy joined the allies in late 1813, a single battery of 152 men and eight guns was formed. Each battery was organised as follows:

1 captain, 2 lieutenants, 1 surgeon, 1 senior pyrotechnicians, 2 pyrotechnicians, 1 sergeant-major, 1 Fourier, 3 sergeants, 5 corporals, 5 bombardiers, 118 cannoneers, 1 fifer, 3 drummers.

The train detachment was commanded by a Lieutenant, and had 1 vetenarian, 1 wagon master, 5 corporals, 2 trumpeters, 77 drivers, 6 officers batmen, 2 smiths, 1 wagon maker and 1 saddlemaker. The train had charge of 6 officers mounts, 10 service mounts, 138 draft horses, 2 7pdr howitzers, 6 6-pdr field guns, 3 howitzer caissons, 10 6pdr caissons, 6 infantry caissons, 1 cavalry caisson, 1 spare howitzer carriage, 1 spare 6-pdr carriage, 4 utility wagons, 1 baggage wagon.

As the campaign of 1813 progressed, the number of batteries raised increased to four, each armed with six 6-pdr and two 7-pdr, and two park columns consisting of 1 train lieutenant, 3 NCO, 5 bombardiers, 1 surgeon, 1 drummer, 24 drivers, 1 saddlemaker, 1 blacksmith, 56 handlanger, 117 horses.

The artillery fought at the battles of Gross-Gorschen (Lutzen), Bautzen and Leipzig, and was overrun on 4th November 1813 by the allies. Hesse-Damrstadt was made to join the allies, the artillery contingent joining the allies being organised as follows:

1 Colonel, 1 Captain, 2 2nd Lieutenants, 1 surgeon, 1 senior pyrotechnician, 2 pyrotechnicians, 1 sergent-major, 1 Fourier, 4 sergeants, 6 corporals, 1 fifer, 3 drummers, 2 bombardiers, 10 first gunners and 116 cannoneers. The train had 98 men,

consisting of 1 Lieutenant, 1 vetenarian, 1 wagon master, 6 corporals, 2 trumpeters, 4 artsians and 83 drivers. The equipment ion service consisted of 2 7-pdr howitzers, 6 6-ppdr, 3 howitzer caissons, 9 6pdr caissons, 8 infantry munitions caissons, 1 artillery requisition cart, 1 field forge, 1 iron and coal caisson, 1 baggage wagon, 24 riding horses and 130 draft horses.

The contingent joined the allies army on March 1814 when an addition sergent, corporal 12 cannoneers, 14 drivers, 24 draft horses, 1 spare howitzer carriage, 1 spare 6-pdr carriage and 4 infantry munition wagons were added. This force saw action against the French at Lyon.

In 1815 when the allies prepared to face Napoleon again, sending a battery of 12 guns (4 7-pdr howitzer and 8 6-pdr) to serve with the Hessian contingent of the Austrian Division of General von Palombini in the Army Corps of Prince von Hessen Homburg. The force did not begin its advance until after waterloo, and they saw no combat.

Equipment.

The Hessian artillery had been formed in 1752 to man regimental artillery pieces, and was only formed into a field artillery regiment on 7th April 1790 and was placed under the command of Major Johann Fischer, replaced by Captain Georg Gottleib Hahn in 1792, who remained as commander until 1814, some sources say 1823.

Captured (French?) gun's given over to the Langrave at the start of 1793 were as follows:

Calibre	Name	Weight (pfund)	Cast date
24 pdr	*Le Bien Venu*	5495	1772
16 pdr	*Le Foyable*	4158	1774
12 pdr	*Le Traductour*	1815	1766
12 pdr	*Le Folatre*	1812	1787
12 pdr	*Le Brulet*	1805	1767
4 pdr	*Le Atlas*	635	1789
4 pdr	*Le Noulier*	604	1767

The regiment was initially of two companies, a third being formed in 1803. In 1793 the regiment had 422men and 264 horses, the train being militariesed in 1796 and consisting of 85men, manning the following guns:

4x 10-pdr howitzers with carriage

8x 7-pdr howitzers with carriage

6x 12-pdr field guns with carriage

2x 6-pdr field guns with carriage

4x 4-pdr French field guns with carriage

11x 3-pdr field guns with carriage.

By 1800 a new system of artillery had been brought into service, the 12-pdr being taken out of service and a new and lighter 6-pdr introduced. The guns were inspired by the French system and were cast at Marxburg under the supervision of Colonel Hahn (1756-1823), who oversaw all construction of field guns and attendant rolling stock. It was he who introduced the Gribeauval designed caisson and 4-pdr, as well as Prussian 7-pdr and 10-pdr howitzers. These Gribeauval caisson was introduced into service In 1754, and were modified in 1764. The ordinary load of a caisson was to not to exceed 1310-lb (595-kg), unless in cases of particular emergency. The interior set up the new caissons was such that they could be altered at will to carry various ammunition types in differing quantities. The large wheels at the rear of the caisson were the same size as the wheel of the 12-pdr, 8-pdr and could be readily changed as they ran on the same axel and were made to the same drawings. The limber at the front of the caisson was to the same design as the limber of the 12-pdr and 8-pdr and could be interchanged at will.

Each battery also had a tool wagon that carried tools for general repairs. All the tools needed to carry out field repairs were carried in one of the caissons of the battery, which in action was kept at the rear with all the other spare wagons.

Smaller tools were kept in a series of wooden boxes inside the caisson along with the other spare items and larger tools. French caissons carried far more ammunition than those of other nations, and as such could not manoeuvre at anything faster than the walk, the caissons also tended to sink in muddy conditions, overturn on un-even ground and were deemed to be too cumbersome for use with horse artillery, whilst the horse artillery of other nations, not being encumbered by caissons could move at the gallop. English, Russian and Polish caissons were of a lightweight design and could manoeuvre with great speed.

The regiment was initially of two companies, a third being formed in 1803. In 1793 the regiment had 422 men and 264 horses, the train being militarised in 1796 and consisting of 85 men, manning the following guns:

> 4x 10-pdr howitzers, 8x 7-pdr howitzers, 6x 12-pdr field guns, 2x 6-pdr field guns, 4x 4-pdr French field guns (old) and 11x 3-pdr field guns

In August 1796 an equipment return lists 4x 10-pdr howitzers, 8x 7-pdr howitzers, 6x 12-pdr with carriages, 2x 6-pdr with carriages, 4x 4-pdr (old) with carriages, 11x 24-pdr.

The train had charge of the following vehicles in 1801:

24x 6-pdr Munition Wagons, 12x Grenade (Shell) Wagons, 1x Ball Wagon, 7x Infantry Munition Wagons, 1x field Forge, 1x Coal wagon, 1x Howitzer Munition wagon, 1x Tool Cart, 1x Augmentationswagon, 2x Tent wagons, 1x bread wagon and 4x officer's baggage wagons.

On 31st December 1801 the Darmstadt Arsenal had the following guns:

10x 6-pdr (old design), 10xx 6-pdr (new design), 7 1-pdr Amusette (very light field gun), 6x 7-pdr Howitzer and 1 x23-pdr Mortar.

The equipment used in the 1806 campaign was as follows:

4 officers mounts, 152 draft horses, 2x 7-pdr howitzers, 6x 6-pdr field guns, 4x 7-pdr howitzer caissons (carrying a total of 216 shells, 32x canister rounds, 184x 1-lb powder bags, 64 ¼-lb powder bags), 10x 6-pdr caissons (carrying a total of 660 round shot, 240 canister), 10 infantry caissons (carrying a total of 46,800 infantry cartridges, 11,520 rifle cartridges, 9,720 musket cartridges, 1,800 pistol cartridges, 900 carbine cartridges and 12,000 flints), 1 field forge, 1 tool wagon, 1 iron and coal wagon, 1 hand tool wagon, 1 officers baggage wagon.

Under the 1807 re-organisation the equipment and train for a battery was as follows:

Material	Number	Train Soldiers	Horses
7-pdr Howitzer	2	4	8
6-pdr	8	16	32
Howitzer Caisson	4	8	16
6-pdr Caisson	16	32	64
Infantry Caisson	9	18	36
Cavalry Caisson	1	2	4
Entrenching tool caisson	1	2	4
Artillery tools	1	2	4
Field Forge	1	2	4
Iron & Coal wagon	1	2	4
Hand tool wagon	1	2	4
Baggage Wagon	1	2	4
Total	50	117	200
Staff Officers		7	6
Wagon master, train etc			7
Total	50	124	213

The train and auxiliary equipment was supervised by a train officer, a wagon master and five train corporals. In addition to this were a farrier, blacksmith and his assistant, a wheelwright and a saddle-maker. At the end of July 1807, Napoleon ordered that Hesse-Darmstadt was to provide an infantry regiment supported by a half battery of guns for service in Spain/ On 21st August 1808, half of the battery of Captain Kuhlman was detached from its garrison duties in

Darmstatdt and despatched to Spain, consisting of 1 2nd lieutenant, 2 corporals, 1 bombardier, 5 first gunners, 58 cannoneers, 2 train corporals, 27 handlnager, 1 offciers servant, some 97 men. The half battery had 1 officers horse, 2 riding horses for the train corporals, and 48 draft horses to pull four 6-pdr, 4 6-pdr caissons with 360 round shot, 120 canister and 12 1-lb powder charges, and 4 infantry caissons containing 11,800 rifle cartridges, 48,920 musket cartridges and 8,000 flints.

In theory in late August 1808, the artillery was to be re-organised on the French principal. One battery saw service in Austria in 1809 which consisted of five 6pdr and 1 7 pdr howitzer, supported by two howitzer caissons (containing in total 108 shells and 16 canister rounds), ten 6-pdr caissons (containing in total 825 round shot, 300 canister rounds), 16 infantry munition wagons, a cavalry munition wagon, a field forge, two artillery tool wagons, an iron and coal wagon for the forge, a hand tool wagon, and a baggage wagon. along with six battalion guns.

For the Russian Campaign, a single battery was prepared for service. The battery had two 7pdr howitzers and six 6pdr guns, served by 103 gunners (1 captain, 2 lieutenants, 1 pyrotechnician, 1 sergent-major, 2 sergents, 4 corpoals,90 gunners and 2 drummers), supported by 90 train troops (1 surgeon, 1 train lieutenant, 1 wagon master, 4 train corporals, 2 trumpeters, 72 drivers, 5 officers batmen, 4 artisans and 1 vetinarian).

This force was totally wiped out in Russia, with only one 6-pdr, one caisson and 3 men returning. In the beginning of 183 a new artillery force was organised., and consisted of four batteries each of two 7pdr howitzer and six 6pdr guns, with 153men per battery. In addition where two reserves of 43men. In 1812 the following equipment was taken:

Equipment	Number
6pdr field gun	6
24pdr Howitzer	2
6pdr Caisson	12
24pdr Howitzer Caisson	4
Infantry caisson	6
Coal wagon	1
Tool cart	1
Field Forge	1
Ammunition Wagon	1
Pontoons	0
Baggage wagons	1
Replacement 6pdr carriage	1
Replacement 24pdr Howitzer carriage	0

6 guns returned to Hesse-Darmstadt in December 1812. Three 6lbs are preserved in the Kremlin museum in Moscow, their details are as follows:

Calibre: 94.0mm, Length (muzzle to base ring) 162.6cm, Weight: 376.6kg

It is unknown if these are the old or new pattern gun. Guns used in 1813 appear to have been primarily the new pattern 6-pdr and 7-pdr introduced in the 1790's. In the 1830's this equipment was replaced with the Valee system of France.

Hesse-Darmstadt Horse Artillery Equipment.

According to Johann Friedrich Hoyer of the Saxon Artillery, Hesse-Darmstadt Horse Artillery made the mistake of utilising 6-pdr of 18 calibres in length weighing some 900lb (409-kg) instead of the better 3-pdr These heavier guns moved at a slower pace and were more cumbersome weapons than the 3-pdr, though they had a longer range and more hitting power. The Hessian artillery had a special limber design, where the pintail was mounted on a wooden block some 40-cm behind the axle, to make limber and un-limbering the gun easier.[37]

---

37 Congreve W, *Note Books* Royal, Artillery Institute, Woolwich

Chapter 7: Kleve-Berg

In 1805, Bavaria released the Duchy of Berg to France and was in return rewarded by the counties of Bayreuth and Ansbach. The Duchy was amalgamated with former Prussian lands and territories conceded by neighbouring states and the throne of the new Grand Duchy was given to marshal Joachim Murat on 15th March 1806. Created 1806, out of 18 minor Rhineland principalities, to give Napoleon's cavalry commander and brother-in-law, Marshal Murat, a realm of his own, Kleve-Berg naturally had no national spirit. After promoting Murat (1808) to King of Naples, Napoleon ruled this state himself through a civilian administrator.

The Kleve-Berg Army had to be created from scratch. Napoleon recalled those citizens serving as mercenaries in other armies (principally the 11th Bavarian Line Infantry Regiment), utilized German-speaking French cadre, and introduced conscription. Suitable officers were hard to find; many were too-rapidly promoted sergeants or German adventurers. Kleve-Berg's contingent was 5,000 (4 infantry and one cavalry regiments and a artillery/engineer battalion), but Napoleon repeatedly called for extra levies-possibly a total of 40,000 men served 1807-1813. (The cavalry became the Regiment of Berg Lancers, with quasi-Imperial Guard status).

The Duchy suffered several losses (1810) or gains (1806, 1808, 1811) of provinces and during this time was divided in four departments, Rhine (partially ceded to France in 1810), Sieg, Ruhr and Ems (ceded to France in 1810), with capital in Düsseldorf.

On 15th July 1808 Murat had become king of Naples and the vacant throne was taken by the Emperor Napoleon himself who gave it in turn to the elder son of the king of Holland, Prince Louis Napoleon, on 3rd March 1809. The new Grand Duke being only four years old, the Emperor became Regent of the Duchy taken in charge by Count Beugnot that will be governor until 1813.

The Berg armed forces took part in the campaign of Prussia in 1807, Spain between 1808 and 1813, Austria in 1809, Russia in 1812 and Germany in 1813.

In 1813 Berg was invaded by the allies and the Prussian territories reverted to their former ruler. The remaining lands were administrated by the Russian General-governor Justus Gruner only to be awarded to Prussia in 1815.

The artillery branch of Grand Duchy army was raised on 29th August 1808 and rose to a single battalion composed of an artillery company, one foot and one horse battery, an engineers company and a train company. The foot battery had 6x 8-pdrs and 2x 6.32inch howitzers, and the horse company 6x 4-pdrs. Its staff consisted of 1 chef de Bataillon, 1 1st Captain, 1 2nd Captain and 2 quarter masters, the two companies had 2 captains, 2 lieutenants and 272 NCO's and men.

The foot artillery company was not to operate as an independent battery, but instead it was to be broken into three regimental batteries which were assigned to the 1st, 2nd and 3rd infantry regiments, and appears to have been organisationally controlled by the decrees of 9th June 1809. Each section of guns was to have 1 sergeant, 1 corporal, 29 gunners, 1 artisan and 10 train troops. A company staff of one lieutenant and one sous-lieutenant was formed as well The staff was changed on 11 February 1811, and had 1 lieutenant, 1 sous-lieutenant, 1 sergeant-major and 1 fourier, each squad was to have 1 sergeant, 1 corporal, 36 gunners, 4 artisans, 26 drivers and 52 horses.

When the Berg artillery force was organised a small artisan company was mobilised as well, to consist of 30 men and one lieutenant, and was moved by a train detachment commanded by a captain, one lieutenant, one sous-lieutenant and 118 drivers.

On March 8th 1811, it was proposed that the following organisation was to be adopted for the batteries:

1 1st captain, 1 2nd captain, 1 1st lieutenant, 1 2nd lieutenant, 1 sergeant-major, 3 sergeants, 1 corporal-fourier, 6 corporals, 3 artisans, 38 cannoneers and 3 drummers.

The train detachment was to have 3 sergeant-majors, 6 corporals, 3 harness makers, 3 blacksmiths, 81 drivers, 3 trumpeters.

The small staff of the foot company was also changed, so that it had 1 1st captain, 1 2nd captain, one 1st lieutenant, and 1 2nd lieutenant, the horse company had a staff of two captains. The artisan company remained unchanged, but a second 2nd lieutenant was added to the train company.

On 24th October 1811 the foot artillery sections were to have 4 officers and 92 men each and a small staff of two officers. By 24th January 1812 the artillery had undergone yet another re-organisation, the staff consisting of one colonel, one lieutenant-colonel, one adjutant-major, on quartermaster, and a surgeon. The light or horse company was to have 1 1st captain, 1 2nd captain, 1 1st lieutenant, 1 2nd lieutenant, 3 sergeants, 1 fourier, 6 corporals, 83 gunners and 2 trumpeters. The foot company was to have 1 1st captain, 1 2nd captain, 1 1st lieutenant, 2 2nd lieutenant, 6 sergeants, 3 fourier, 6 corporals, 4 artisans, 108 gunners and 3 drummers. The artisan company remained unchanged but the train company was expanded, having 1 1st captain, 1 2nd captain, 1 1st lieutenant, 2 2nd lieutenant, 1 sergent-major, 6 sergeants, 1 fourier, 10 corporals, 196 drivers, 2 harness makers, 2 blacksmith, 6 trumpeters and 374 horses.

On 16th January 1813, the artillery battalion had 2 officers, 1 sergeant-major, 2 sergeants, 3 corporals, 18 1st gunners, 30 cannoneers, 10 artisans and 1 drumer, manning 4x 6-pdrs, 6x 6-pdr caissons, 4 infantry caissons, 1 field forge and a powder cart. The light artillery between 16 January and 27 April 1813 as having 1 chef d'Escadron, 1 2nd captain, 1 2nd lieutenant, 1 sergeant-major, 4 sergents, 4 corporals, 10 1st gunners, 40 gunners 10 artisans and 2 trumpeters, manning 1 howitzer, 2 6-pdr, 3 howitzer caissons, 3 6-pdr caissons, 1 infantry caisson, 1 field forge and 1 power wagon.

Between 16th January and 1st April 1813 the train company is recorded as having 1 1st captain, 1 2nd lieutenant, 1 sergeant-major, 3 sergeants, 3 corporals, 81 drivers, 1 trumpeter, 1 harness maker and 1 blacksmith.

The decree of 29th January 1813 had raised a fourth foot artillery section of one lieutenant, one sergeant, one corporal and 18 gunners. Its purpose is unclear.

1st April 1813 saw the light artillery having four officers an d 96 men,By July 1813 the light artillery had been rebuilt and equipped with two howitzers and four 6-pdr guns, being assigned to the French Imperial Guard artillery pool The train detachment had 3 officers and 100 drivers, the artisan company one officer and 30men, the depot having 12 officers and 30 men. In 1814 when Berg was restored to Prussia a foot battery proper and a half battery or horse artillery was raised.

Equipment.

The foot battery was equipped with 6x 8-pdr guns and 2x 6.32-inch howitzers, of French manufacture. The horse battery was equipped with 6x 4 pounder guns. It too was annihilated during the Russian campaign. In 1812 the army of Berg fielded eight French 6-pdrs and four 24-pdr French howitzers. In addition to this was the Regimental Artillery, organised by the decree of 11th February 1811, which issued 2 field guns, 6 caissons, 1 field forge, 4 rations carts, 1 ambulance and 1 equipment caisson to each infantry regiment. A further decree of 25th June 1811 allocated 2x 6-pdr guns to each regiment and an extra caisson. It appears that the 4th regiment's equipment was removed and issued to the horse artillery which was to have 4x 6-pdr, 4x 6-pdr caissons, 2x howitzers, 2x howitzer caissons, 4x infantry caissons, and 1x park wagon.

On 16th January 1813, the foot artillery was armed with 4x 6-pdrs, 6x 6-pdr caissons, 4x infantry caissons, 1x field forge and 1 powder wagon. By July the Horse artillery battery had been reformed, and equipped with 4x 6-pdr and two howitzers, and was assigned to the French Imperial Guard. Regimental artillery was reformed. Guns appear to have been of French pattern.

French M1808 field forge, the same type as used in Kleve-Berg. (La Garde Imperiale).

The horse artillery was re-raised in January 1813 and took part in the 1813 campaign in the Imperial Guard Artillery pool. Prussian rulers organized a foot battery and a half horse battery in 1814. They would be assigned in 1815 to the Prussian army as 37th foot battery and 20th horse battery.

French M1808 6-pdr field gun, the same type as used by the Kleve-Berg Artillery in 1813. (La Garde Imperiale).

Chapter 8: Mecklenburg -Schwerin

Until 1795, three battalions served with the Dutch Army. In 1808, joined the Confederation of the Rhine. Initially, the artillery consisted of two regimental guns attached to the Mecklenburg Schwerin contingent.

A foot battery was raised in 1809 armed with six French guns under command of a French officer. The organisation was as follows:

> 1 Major, 1 Captain, 1 Lieutenant, 1 2nd Lieutenant, 4 Seargeants, 1 Warrant Officer, 8 Corporals, 1 Quartermaster, 1 drummer, 64 gunners (1st Class) and 32 gunners.

In July 1813 when they joined the allies, the foot battery was re-equipped with British 7-pdr ship howitzers, Swedish 6-pdr, 2 old Mecklenburg 6-pdr, two ammunition wagons (50 rounds and 50 charges each), one shell wagon and one baggage wagon. The company had one 1st Lieutenant and 37 NCOs & men. By 1814, the artillery company had been augmented to 1 captain, 1 1st Lieutenant, 1 2nd Lieutenant, 11 NCOs, 2 drummers, 69 gunners, 1 surgeon and 34 horses.

A foot battery is raised in 1809 armed with six guns under command of a French officer. In 1813, these were re-equipped with British and Swedish guns.

Chapter 9: Saxony.

The history of the Saxon Army is very complex, and can be touched on only briefly here. Although the relationship between Prussia and Saxony was somewhat cool during the Revolutionary Wars, in 1806 Saxony fought as a forced ally of Prussia, but the 20,000 Saxons could not save the Prussian Army from defeat at Jena and Auerstadt. In contrast to the flight of the Prussians, contemporary accounts describe the Saxon units retreating from the battlefield in perfect order with bands playing.

The electorate of Saxony was raised to a Kingdom by Napoleon, and the new King Friedrich August entered into an Alliance with Napoleon, being obliged to contribute 20,000men if called to do so. This alliance came to an end at Leipzig in October 1813, the same year that the Saxon Guard Grenadiers became part of the French Imperial Guard. At Wagram, the Saxon troops suffered 40% casualties.

The artillery was formed in 1766 had a small staff that included a director from the artillery staff, fourteen instructors and four assistant NCO's. In 1791, the Saxon artillery had 12 companies (1584 men).

Regimental Staff (15 men)

    1 Chef, 1 Oberst, 2 Oberstlieutenants, 2 Majors, 2 Adjutants, 1 Quartermaster, 1 Auditeur, 1 Ober-Feldscheer, 1 Staff-Fourier, 1 Staff-Feldscheer, 1 Provost

Artillery Company (132 men)

    1 Captain, 1 1st Lieutenant, 2 2nd Lieutenant., 1 Stückjunker, 1 Feldscheer, 1 Sergeant, 1 Feuerwerker-Corporal, 3 Feuerwerker, 1 Fourier, 9 Corporals, 2 drummers, 3 carpenters, 1 Mineur, 19 senior gunners and 86 gunners. In 1797 each company received an additional Feuerwerker, Corporal, 4 senior gunners and 18 gunners.

On 4th February 1802, the horse battery was planned but not until 16th March 1806 was it ordered to be formed and mobilised on 1 May 1806.

The Saxon army of 1806 was an awkward imitation of the Prussian Army of 1786, Most senior officers were elderly and objected to any modernisation that Saxony's alliance with France required. The artillery arm of Saxony was formed in 1766 with a small staff that included a director from the artillery staff, fourteen instructors and four assistant NCO's. The guns were designed by Rouvroy, and had a unique elevating system, allowing some 10degree elevation and 5degrees of depression. The army had light and heavy 4-pdr, 8-pdr, 12-pdr, and 24-pdr field guns. The organisation of the Saxon Artillery for the Jena campaign was as follows:

Commandant: Oberst OSL Rouvroy
Commandant du Parc: Major Van Bünau
    1st Battery. Captain Bonniot (6 heavy 12-pdr & 2 8-pdr Howitzers)
    2nd Battery: Captain Hausmann II (6 heavy 8-pdr & 2 8-pdr howitzers)
    3rd Battery: Captain Ernst (6 8-pdr 2 8-pdr howitzers)
    4th Battery: Captain Tüllmann (6 4-pdr Granatstücke & 2 heavy 4-pdr)
    5th Battery: Captain Kotzsch (6 4-pdr Granatstücke & 2 heavy 4-pdr)
    6th Battery: Captain Hoyer (2 4-pdr Granatstücke & 6 heavy 4-pdr)
    Horse Battery: 1st Lieutenant Van Grossmann (2 4-pdr Granatstücke 6 heavy 4-pdr)
    50 regimental guns.

The organisation of the Saxon Artillery for the Jena campaign was as follows:

Foot Battery in 1806 had 124 men:
> 1 Captain, 1 1st Lieutenant, 1 2nd Lieutenant, 1 Sergeant, 1 Oberfeuerwerker, 1 Fourier, 1 surgeon, 10 Feuerwerker-Corporals, 2 drummers, 2 Zimmerleute, 3 Ouvriers, 100 gunners.

Horse battery of 1806 had 97 Men and 91 horses:
> 1 1st Lieutenant, 2 2nd Lieutenant, 1 Stückjunker, 1 Sergeant, 2 Feuerwerker, 1 Fourier, 1 surgeon, 6 corporals, 2 Trumpeter, 20 senior gunners and 60 gunners.

Train of 1806
> 1 Wagenmaster, 26 drivers with 52 horses and 4 Handwerker

The artillery fought at Schleiz, Saalburg, Saalfeld and Jena where it lost 3 officers and 9 men killed in action, 8 Officiers and 95 men wounded and 12 Officers and 782 men captured.

In French Service.

After Jena-Auerstädt, Saxony changed sides and on 11th December 1806, Napoleon raised the electorate of Saxony to a Kingdom upon joining the Confederation of the Rhine. By 24 December 1806 had mobilised 300 gunners manning two batteries of 4 8-pdr and 4-pdr Granatstücke commanded by Captains Kirsten and Semder were mobilised as part of the Marshal Mortier's VIII Corps of the Grande Armee. The Saxon artillery served in Marshal Lefebvre's X Corps at Danzig. During the battle of Pillau (16 March 1807), the Saxons were brigaded with the Polish Artillery. In 1808, these batteries were part of the garrison of Warsaw, Poland.

The 1809 war against Austria, saw the Saxon artillery being brigaded with the Polish artillery commanded by General Poniatowski, the organisation being as follows:

    1st Division 9 Corps:

        Heavy Battery: Captain Hoyer (4x 8lb, 2x 8inch howitzers)

        Light Battery: Captain Benniot (4x 8lb, 2x 8inch howitzers)

    2nd Division 9 Corps

        Heavy Battery: Captain Coudray (4x 8lb, 2x 8inch howitzers)

Light Battery: Captain Huthsteiner (2x 8lb, 2x 8inch howitzers)

On 2nd April 1809, a second horse battery (3 light 8-pdr & 1 4pd. Granatstück) under Capitain Grossmann was created. On 17 May 1809, the Horse battery commanded by 1st Lieutenant Hiller was formed at Linz with 2 light 8-pdr guns from the Huthsteiner Battery and 2 light 8-pdr guns from the Reserve Park.

At Wagram (5-6 July 1809) the Saxon Artillery expended 2337 rounds for the cost of 12 gunners and 41 horses were killed; 1 officer, 15 gunners and 6 horses wounded, 3 men deserted; 9 guns, 6 howitzers, 2 limbers and 9 ammunition wagons were destroyed.[38] At Wagram in 1809, 12 gunners were killed, 1 officer was wounded along with 15 gunners. 3 men deserted, 9guns and 6 howizters were destroyed and 41horses were also killed.

In Poland the batteries of Capitain Kotzsch and Semder a total of 14 guns fought at Raszyn.

---

38 Pigeard A., "L'artillerie a Pied Saxonne 1806-1813," *Tradition Magazine,* 16, 23-28

The poor performance of the Saxon Artillery and the heavy cumbersome and increasingly out dated material resulted in the artillery being re-organsied by an Imperial Decree of 20th February 1810 on French lines. The decree created 16 companies, totalling some 78 officers and 1771men. New guns were produced, using the same calibres as the French, in total 56 guns of the System of Year 11 were supplied to Saxony. However official inventories show that the light 4-pdr was used as regimental artillery.

In 1810 the foot artillery was separated from the horse artillery and was formed into a foot artillery regiment of 16 companies (1849 men), the organisation being as follows:

    Staff (24 men)

        1 Oberst, 2 Oberstlieutenants, 3 Majors, 7 Adjutants, 1 Regimental Quartermaster, 1 Auditeur, 1 Senior Regimental Surgeon, 1 Stabssekretaire, 6 surgeons, 1 Provost

    Of each company:

        1 Captain, 1 1st Lieutenant, 2 2nd Lieutenants, 1 Sergeant, 1 Oberfeuerwerker, 3 Feuerwerker, 1 Fourier, 6 Corporals, 2 Drummers, 16 senior gunners and 80 gunners.

The regiment was divided in three brigades to 5 companies each. Each brigade manned four batteries and had an Artillery Park. The horse artillery brigade had two batteries organised as follows:

Staff (2 men)
1 Major, 1 Adjutant

Each battery (121 men and 113 Horses)
1 Captain, 1 1st Lieutenant, 2 2nd Lieutenant, 1 Sergeant, 2 Feuerwerker, 1 Fourier, 8 Korporals, 1 surgeon, 2 Trumpeter, 1 Schmied, 20 senior gunner and 80 gunners.

Handwerker-Kompanie (artillery workers)
1 Kaptain, 1 Lieutant, 32 Schmiede (blacksmith), 6 Schlosser (metalworker), 1 Büchsenmacher (weaponmaker), 1 Büchsenschäfter (wood worker for muskets), 12 Sattler (saddler), 12 Wagner (waggon worker) Total 66 men.

In 1811, the first artillery regulation for Saxony was issued, and it decree that each company was to be a battery with the following equipment:

4 guns, 2 howitzers, 2 wagons for each gun and 3 wagons for each howitzer. From these wagons the battery provided 4 gun wagons and 4 howitzer wagons to the so called

"Parc Intermediaire". So each piece in the battery had only 1 wagon. Each gun was served by 1 NCO, 1 senior gunners and 7 gunners with 1 senior gunner and 1 gunner with ammunition wagon.

During the 1812 campaign, the Saxons formed part of 7th Corps, under the command of Lt-Colonel Van Hoyer. In the campaign 1 officer and 146men killed, 12guns were destroyed and 167 horses were killed. In the campaign they lost 1 officer, 146 men and 167 horses killed with 12 guns destroyed.

For the 1812 campaign Saxony provided two Divisions (21st and 22nd) to VII Corps with a total artillery strength of 58 Officiers, 1803 men (including artillery train) and 56 guns. All batteries had 4 6-pdr and 2 8-pdr howitzer. The regimental guns were the old "Schnellfeuergeschütze" [literally quick fire guns] that had been used as regimental guns from 1806. The Artillery fought at Kobryn, Pruszana, Podubny, Lesna, and Biala. On 28 Oct 1812, the artillery had 57 officers, 1304 men and 1139 horses. The next fights were at Wolkowysk and Kalisch.

VII Corps: Artillery Commander Oberstlieutnant Hoyer
21st Division: Artillery Commander Major Grossmann

4th Foot (Captain Brause) 4 Officers and 115 men
1st horse (Captain Roth) 4 Officers and 156 men
Regimental guns for 3 IR) 3 Offc. 186 men
Division park   3 Offc. 110 men

22nd division: Artillery Commander Major Auenmüller
   3rd Foot (Captain Bonniot) 4 Officers and 114 men
   2nd horse (Captain Hiller) 4 Officers and 169 men. The 2nd horse fought with the Saxon heavy cavalry brigade at Borodino and were totally lost between near Wilna (17-19 November 1812).
   Regimental guns for 2 IR (2 Officers and 124 men)
Division Park (unknown)

Reserve artillery (Major Hoyer)
   2nd Foot   Kaptain Sontag   4 Offc. 114 men
   1st Foot   Kaptain Rouvroy   4 Offc. 115 men

To IX Corps serving in Danzig, Saxony provided 2 Prussian 3-pdr to serve as regimental artillery for the Rechten Infantry Regiment.

To XI Corps, One 6-pdr battery under Captain Essenius. This battery was part of the 34th divison Morand and captured at Lüneburg (2 April 1813).

In the 1812 campaign they lost 1 officer, 146 men and 167 horses killed with 12 guns destroyed. In 1813, the remnants of the Saxon was combined into a single division with 2 batteries and a Divisional Artillery Park.
    1st 6-pdr Battery (Captain Kühnel)
    2nd 6-pdr Battery (Captain Rouvroy II)

At the beginning of August 1813, the Saxon Army was reorganised and rebuilt into the 24th and 25th Divisions. The artillery now had 36 officers, 1317 men and 52 pieces.

24th (Saxon) Division: Artillery Commander Major Roth
    1st 6-pdr Battery (Captain Kühnel) of 4 officers, 168 men and 8 pieces
    2nd 6-pdr Battery (Captain Rouvroy II) of 4 officers, 179 men and 8 pieces
    Division Park of 2 officers and 95 men.

25th (Saxon) Division: Artillery Commander Major Gau
    3rd 6-pdr Battery (Captain Dietrich) of 4 officers, 164 men and 8 pieces.

4th 6-pdr Battery (Captain Zandt) of 4 officers, 173 men and 8 pieces.

Division Park of 2 officers and 73 men.

Saxon Cavalry

1st Horse Battery (Captain Birnbaum) of 4 officers, 172 men and 6 pieces

2nd Horse Battery (Captain Probsthayn) of 4 officers, 147 men and 6 pieces.

Reserve artillery

12-pdr Battery (Captain Rouvroy I) of 3 officers, 206 men and 8 pieces.

Main Artillery Park (Major Grossmann) of 3 officers and 266 men

Losses at Grossbeeren were 20 men killed and , wounded were 2 Offcers 17 men. The missing included 3 Offcer, 149 men and 215 horses, along 7 pieces and 53 wagons. Losses at Dennewitz were 1 men killed , 22 men wounded, 1 officer , 135 men, 214 horses, 12 pieces and 40 wagons were listed as missing.

On 8th September 1813, due to attrition, the 24th and 25th (Saxon) Divisions were reduced to 22 officers, 826 men, 607 horses and 33 pieces with 3 pieces sent to the fortress Torgau:

    24th Division
        1st 6-pdr Battery (Dietrich) with 8 pieces
    25th Division
        2nd 6-pdr Battery (Zandt) with 8 pieces
    Saxon Cavalry
        2nd Horse Battery (Probsthayn) with 4 pieces
    Reserve Artillery
        12-pdr Battery (Rouvroy I) with 6 pieces
        1st Horse Battery (Birnbaum) with 4 pieces

By October 1813, the Reserve Park received 8 "out of order" pieces and on 16th October 1813, these together with the main artillery park and most of the divisional train was sent to Torgau.

With the Allies

On 17th October 1813 the artillery had a 6-pdr Foot Battery (5 Officers, 188 men, 128 horses and 8 pieces), 12-pdr Foot Battery (4 officers, 140 men, 120 horses and 6 pieces), two 6-pdr Horse Batteries (6 officers, 178 men, 121 horses, 8 pieces combined). Three pieces were lost on in action 18 October. At 17:30 on the 18th October, 19 pieces went over the Allies at Leipzig. At this time the artillery had the following organisation:[39]

> 1st Infantry Brigade:
>> Captain Dietrich (6 6-pdr 2 howitzers)
>
> Light Cavalry Brigade:
>> Captain Von Birnbaum (3 6-pdr 1 howitzer)
>
> Reserve Artillery:
>> 2nd Horse Artillery Battery Captain Probthyan (3 6-pdr 1 howitzer)
>>
>> 1st Foot Battery: Captain von Rouvroy (4 12-pdr 2 howitzers),
>>
>> 2nd Foot battery: Captain Zandt (6 6-pdr 2 howitzers).

On 19 October 1813, the Saxon artillery withdrew to garrison duties at Glogau, their field artillery being placed in the arsenal there.

---

39 Pigeard A "L'artillerie a Pied Saxonne 1806-1813," *Tradition Magazine*, 16, 23-28

Equipment.

Hoyer M 1772.

In 1772, Colonel J G Hoyer director of the Artillery School assisted by Major Raabe redesigned the artillery of the duchy. This was not a completely new system, as the 8-pdr and 12-pdr guns tubes (light and heavy) were retained but mounted on new carriages, with an unique elevating system permitting some 10 degree elevation and 5 degrees of depression, and was apparently an improved design of the Hanoverian system. Hoyer and Raabe also designed a light quick firing 4-pdr, single 24-pdr for siege and position work as well as a 4-pdr grenade thrower. The caissons for the 4-pdr grenade thrower and 4-pdr field gun carried the ball and ammunition separately, whilst the ammunition for the 8-pdr and 12-pdr was carried in a caisson not dissimiliar to Gribeauval designs.

The Saxon Old Ordnance were of 16 calibres long except the heavy 4-pdr that was 21 calibres long. The 8-pdr howitzer had a tube length of 6 calibres and the 4-pdr Granatstück 9 calibres. As it fired only 4-pdr case shot grenades, it was able to carry 50-60 rounds in its ammunition chest. Its canister, containing 28 balls of eight 'lot' each, was effective at a range of 756 paces.[40] When Horse Artillery was assigned for outpost duty, it was suggested that none or only a few guns should be used, but instead utilise the already mentioned 'Granatstück', because of the length of its tube comparable to the light howitzer, as it was more advantageous, and was as accurate as cannon. The chance of grenades failing to explode was very small, when care was taken in the preparation of the fuse. The grenades mentioned appear to be case shot grenades. In 1780 Hoyer introduced a new limber design, with a limber box.

Gun	Calibre	Tube Length	Tube weight	Carriage weight	Limber weight
12-pdr heavy	115 mm	184 cm	1121 kg	740 kg	313 kg
12-pdr light	115 mm	184 cm	794 kg	640 kg	297 kg
8-pdr heavy	100.6 mm	161 cm	748 kg	533 kg	239 kg
8-pdr light	100.6mm	161 cm	523 kg	462 kg	220 kg
4-pdr heavy	78.7 mm	165 cm	420 kg	426 kg	200 kg
4-pdr light	78.7 mm	126 cm	313 kg	426 kg	200 kg
8inc howitzer	154.8 mm	93 cm	398 kg	878 kg	193 kg
Granatstück	154.8 mm	124 cm	325 kg	491 kg	321 kg

The bores were 16 calibres long, though the heavy 4-pdr was some 21 calibres long. The 8pound howitzer had a bore and chamber length of 6 calibres, the 4pound Granatstück 9 calibres.

---

40 Hoyer 1798 opcit

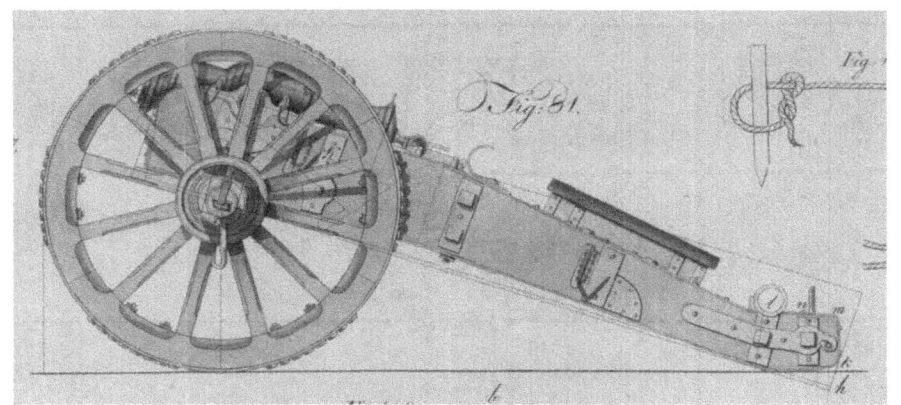

Hoyer howitzer carriage (S H Smith).

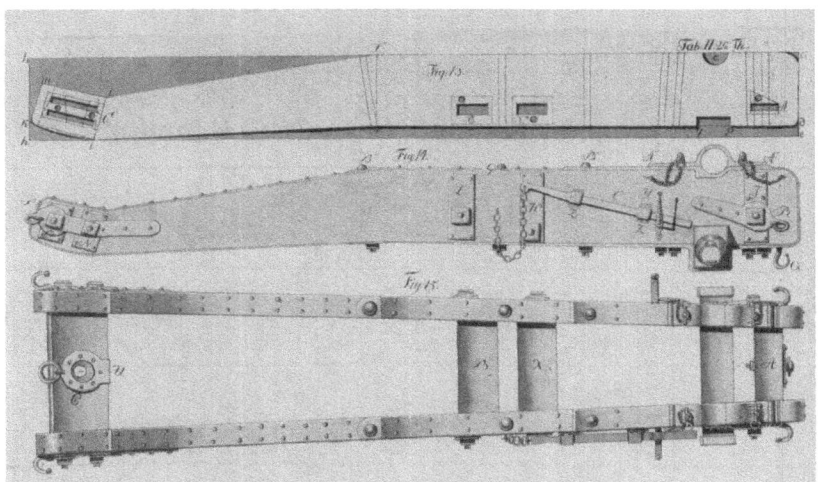

Hoyer 8-pdr gun carriage.(S H Smith).

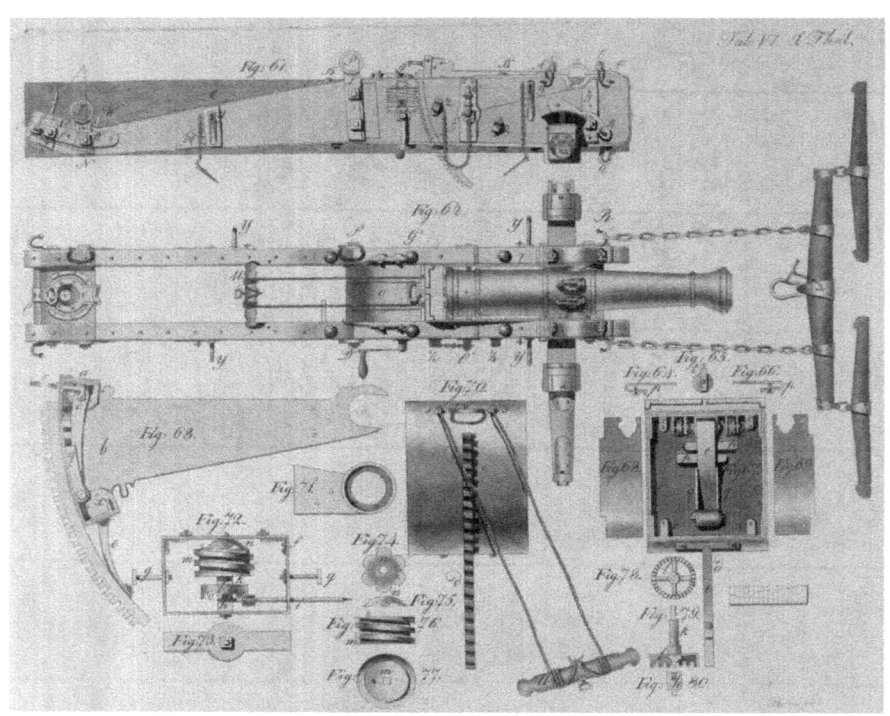

Hoyer quick fire or light 4-pdr. (S H Smith).

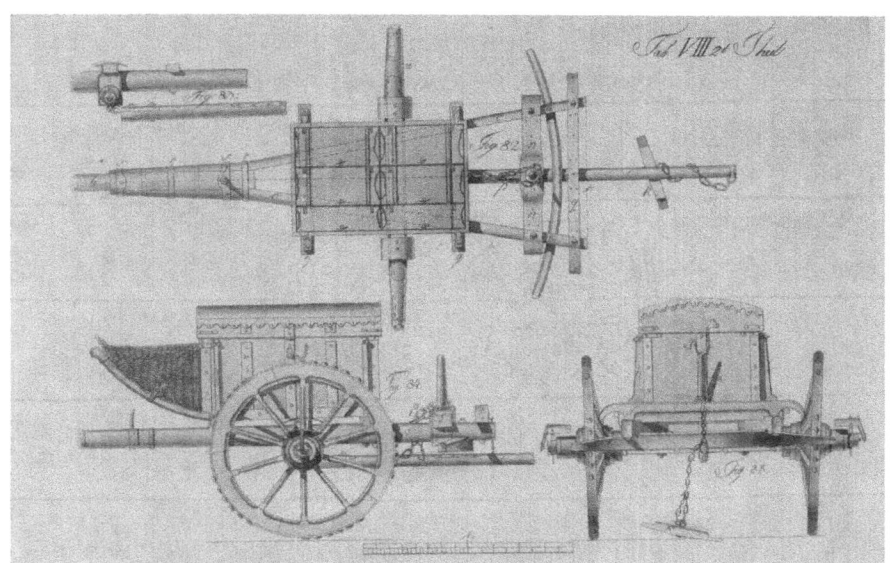

Hoyer 1780 limber design, apparently for use with all calibres of field guns (S H Smith).

Hoyer ammunition caisson. This design, made with wicker sides was copied off the Austrian design. It replaced the solid bodied designs based on the Gribeauval system as it was lighter and easier to move. (S H Smith).

Raabe M1811

The artillery staff of Saxony lightened the gun carriages, and introduced new 6-pdr and 12-pdr field gun as well as a new 8-inch howitzer. The gun tubes had a bore length of 18 calibres, and the

Saxon M1811 12-pdr as preserved in Copenhagen. (S H Smith).

howitzers 7 calibres. The 4-pdr grenade thrower was retained but the gun tube was modified to make it lighter. The 24-pdr field gun was assigned to the siege train. A unique feature of these guns was the replacement of the back weight with a handle, suppression of the reinforcements, and the gun carriages were made with all bronze fittings rather than the iron as used most commonly. New caissons were introduced as well as a new training manual.

One aspect of the M1811 reforms was the use of two wheel sizes, small for limbers (113-cm diameter) and heavy and light large (119-cm diameter) for the guns and rear wheels of vehicles. All guns had a loading gauge of 113-cm

Gun	Calibre	Tube length	Tube weight	Carriage weight	Limber weight
12-pdr	115 mm	207 cm	585 kg	640 kg	300 kg
6-pdr	92.6 mm	167 cm	392 kg	530 kg	200 kg
8 inch howitzer	154.8 mm	80 cm	320 kg	790 kg	300 kg

With the reconstruction of the army came in 1813 new ammunition wagons were introduced, their contents being as follows:
      12-pdr ammunition wagon (65 ball, 10 canister in 15 boxes)
      6-pdr ammunition wagon (130 balls, 20 canister in 15 boxes)

Infantry cartridge wagon (15840 cartridges in 22 boxes and 2400 musket flints)

Cavalry cartridge wagon (18000 cartridges in 22 boxes and 2500 musket flints)

Ordnance Inovators: Saxony

Johann Gotfreid Hoyer (1726-1802)

Born in Dresden, entered the Saxon artillery in 1746, and had risen to rank of Major General by 1792. Director of the Artillery School since 1766 and director of Artillery Manufacturing and design from 1772. Introdcued the 4-pdr grenade thrower, 4-pdr quick fire gun, the unique chain driven elevating system, new mortars, new field gun carriages, new munition wagons and introduced new methods of munition production. The two calibres of 8-pdr, 12-pdr and 24-pdr were retained from the previous system. In 1780 a new limber design was introduced.

Raabe

Assistant to Hoyer in the 1770's and re-designer of the Saxon Artillery in 1810/1811.

Chapter 10: Westphalia

Westphalia was an 1807 creation - a combination of Hesse-Cassel, Brunswick, portions of Hanover, and Prussia's Rhineland principalities. It ran eastward from the Dutch frontier across the southern border of Denmark; on the east it half-encircled Berlin. Napoleon conceived it as an anchor for the northern end of the Confederation's territories, a satellite kingdom that would both check Prussia's westwards encroachments and bring an example of modern society and the rights of man to backward, feudal-minded northern Germany. Its contingent was 25,000 men. Napoleon made his youngest brother, Jerome, its king.

This new state showed promise, but the constant wars and their increasing demands for men and money did not give it opportunity to really establish itself. Jerome was intelligent, brave, even courageous on occasion, full of good humour and good intentions. Unfortunately, he also was irresponsible - a playboy king, carelessly extravagant, dissolute, wanting instant gratification of every whim, full of pretensions to high command for which he had neither training, experience, nor competence.

Jerome's army had a solid core in the "Hessian Legion"- Hesse-Cassel troops that had served with the French in 1806. Napoleon intended that it be organized deliberately, only 12,500 being mobilized during the first few years. Jerome, however, rushed the matter, producing a large, raw army that-in part because of his own frivolity-made a weak showing in 1809, and a mediocre one in 1812. Jerome fielded a new army in 1813, but-except for some regiments on garrison duty-it was soon riddled by desertions. The Allies absorbed its remnants. During the Russian campaign, the horse artillery was commanded by Captain Lemaitre and consisted of 165men in the 1st brigade of the 24th Division of 8th Corps of the Grande Armee. The train was commanded by Captain Von Pfuhl, and consisted of 133men.

In 1808 the Kingdom had 18 field guns, increasing to 40 filed guns and 16 howitzers in 1811 accompanied by 400 train horses, the organisation being as follows:

Regimental Staff: 2 colonels, 2 bataillonschef, 1 train commander, 1 adjutant major, 1 paymaster, 1 1st class surgeon, 1 2nd class surgeon, 2 adjutants, 1 veterinarian, 1 assistant veterinarian, 1 drum major, 1 staff trumpeter, 1 depot quartermaster, 2 depot artisans.

Foot Company: 1 captain commandant, 1 2nd captain, 1 1st lieutenant, 1 2nd lieutenant, 1 sergent-major, 3 sergeants, 1 fourier, 3 corporals, 1 artificer, 30 1st gunners, 60 cannoneers, 2 drummers.

Horse Company: 1 captain commandant, 1 2nd captain, 1 1st lieutenant, 1 2nd lieutentant, 1 sergeant major, 3 sergeants, 1 corporal-fourier, 3 corporals, 3 artificers, 28 1st gunners, 45 cannoneers, 2 saddlemakers, 4 trumpeters.

Train Company: 1 1st lieutenant, 1 2nd lieutenant, 1 sergeant-major, 3 sergeants, 1 fourier, 6 corporals, 28 1st drivers, 52 drivers, 2 blacksmiths, 2 saddlemakers, 2 trumpeters.

The sapper and artisan companies were organised like the foot artillery companies but were commanded by only two officers, the gunners being replaced by either 105 sappers or artisans.

Originally Westphalia used the French 1791 d'Urtubie drill manual and regulations, but these were replaced by the 'Collections des lois arêtes, et reglements actuellement en vigeur, sur les differents service de l'artilleire' which was puiblished in Paris in 1812.

Westphalian batteries had six guns, either 4x 6-pdr and two howitzers or 4x 12-pdrs and 2x howitzers, divided into three two gun sections, both howitzers being brigaded together each section being commanded by a sergeant. Each section was supplied with two caissons. The train vehicles were commanded by the 2nd Captain, and two train NCO's served as the leader and direction NCO's

Equipment.

Westphalia inherited equipment from Brunswick, Hannover and Hesse-Kassel, from which the Kingdom was created. The material inherited from Hesse-Kassel consisted of 16 3pdr and 2 1pdr guns.

In December 1807 four batteries of guns were established, using Russian ordnance. These guns were of the 1805 Arakcheev system.

By 1809 6 companies of foot artillery had been raised and one of horse artillery, all being armed with four 6pdr and two 7pdr howitzers, (a total of 28x 6pdr and 16x 7pdr howitzers). These had all been designed by French General Allix. The equipment used during the 1812 campaign was apparently of French design:

Equipment	Number
6pdr field gun	26
24pdr Howitzer	8
12pdr field gun	4
6pdr Caisson	41
24pdr Howitzer Caisson	25
12pdr caisson	12
Infantry caisson	23
Coal wagon	1
Tool cart	9
Field Forge	11
Ammunition Wagon	1
Pontoons	5
Baggage wagons	11
6pdr ammunition: canister rounds	1,020
24pdr Howitzer canister rounds	48
6pdr ammunition drawn from caissons	4,325
24pdr howitzer shells with powder charge	1,472
24pdr howitzer powder bags	1,050
Replacement 6pdr carriage	4
Replacement carriage 12pdr	0
Replacement carriage 24pdr howitzer	0

Surviving guns in the Kremlin and elsewhere are of two types, Prussian style with no handles or French gribeaval style. Both types are of identical calibre (94mm), weight 368.55 Kg and bore length of 16 calibres. Two surviving howitzers in the Kremlin have a calibre of 152mm, a bore length of 101.6cm and weigh 298.4kg.

Chapter 11: Württemberg

An initial member of the Confederation, Württemberg had already been a French ally, providing troops during Napoleon's 1805 campaign. Its ruler, Duke Friedrich was grossly fat, needing - so it was said - specially trained Percherons for saddle horses, but he was also a highly intelligent, iron-willed, and grimly efficient despot.

Friedrich was thoroughly military minded, relentlessly modernizing and increasing his army. He was the first German ruler to institute an effective form of conscription (1806). Though a rigid disciplinarian, he looked after his soldiers, and opened his officer corps to qualified non-nobles. His contingent was 12,000 men.

The army he created was undoubtedly the best of any in the Confederation of the Rhine tough, hard-marching, always aggressive, capable of looking after itself.

The first permanent formation of artillery was built under Duke Karl Alexander, when he ordered to instruct selected people in Handling and Usage of guns (cannons and mortars) in 1734.

In 1736 an artillery-company was formed and from then, the artillery was regarded as military service and no longer as guild occupation, and became more professional. July of 1758 saw Duke Carl Eugen being ordered to set up an artillery-batallion. Since 1759 engineer-officers belonged to the artillery, as did the so-called "Conducteurs" and "Guides".

After the Seven Years' War the artillery was reduced by one company. The artillery-battalion consisted of 5 companies. As common in the most armies, there was given auxiliaries from the infantry-regiments to the artillery. Just as common, smaller calibres was attached to the infantry-regiments. The headquarters of the artillery consisted of 13 men:

> 1 Oberst (colonel),1 Major (major),1 Commissär (Officer appointed to execute financial affairs),1 Adjutant (adjutant),1 Feldscher (surgeon,)1 Pauker (kettle-drummer),6 Hautboists (hautboists)1 Profoß (Provost)

The 5 company's consisted altogether of 240 men. Every company was commanded by 3 officiers and had 45 NCOs and privates, toatalling 48 men. 2 of the companies were of artillery, 2 companies of workmen and 1 company of miners and bombardiers.

In December 1775 the corps was raised to a total of eight foot companies, the first being known as the Grenadier Company, the remaining companies were known by the names of their commanders:

Grenadier co.	Major Von Zobels
2nd Co.	Hauptmann Schide
3rd Co.	Hauptmann Obernitz
4th Co.	Hauptmann Fischer
5th Co.	Hauptmann Walter
6th Co.	Hauptmann Massenbach
7th Co.	Hauptmann d'Obrenils
8th Co.	Hauptmann von Mylius.

The organisation was reduced back to five companies in 1777. 1783 saw the formation of a horse artillery company attached to the Ducal Guard, and served four 3pdr. By 1788 it became fully organised and incorporated into the Guard:

> 1 Colonel Sergeant, 1 Staff Captain, 4 Lieutenants, 2 Sergeants, 1 Quartermaster, 8 Corporals, 61 gunners, 8 drivers.

According to Saxon Artillery officer Johnann Hoyer the Württemberg horse artillery at this period had the following concept:

> they utilised 3lb and 6lb cannon, each with two horses, and a driver ['Fuhrmann'] with four horses and two drivers ['Fuhrleuten']. The latter are in fact artillerymen, armed with a sabre the same as the others. The gun crew is mounted, and consists for the 3lb of an NCO and five gunners, for the 6lb of an NCO and eight gunners. The horse-holder is seated on the limber. When the gun would have to deploy, the horse-holder jumps off the limber to hold the horses of the crew. Limbering is executed as usual, the horse-holder climbing on the limber again. The Duke of Württemberg has a company of this horse artillery with his guards [Garde-Legion'].

> The disadvantages of this concept are obvious. The mounted crew-members will have to find themselves a safe spot to dismount before they arrive at their position, but they cannot leave their horses before the cannon has halted at the right position, the horse-holder has jumped down from the limber, and has walked to the horses to take over the reins. When limbering again, the cannon has to stop, until the crew has mounted again, and the horse-holder is then seated on the limber.

This was changed in 1808 when a new wurst ammunition wagon was adopted which allowed all the gun crew to ride on it, as well as two further gunners being able to ride on the semi wurst gun carriage, inspired by the Austrian system.

The arsenal at Ludwigsburg in December 1783 had the following pieces of ordnance:

20x howitzers, 6x stone throwers, 12x 12-pdr, 12x 6-pdr, 50x 3-pdr in Brass, 4x 3-pdrs in Iron, 12x Falconets, 6x Jager pieces.

In May 1792 the artillery sent to fight France in the war of the First Coalition was armed with:

5x heavy 12-pdr, 2x light 12-pdr, 1x heavy 6-pdr, 4x light 6-pdr

This organisation had its equipment changed continually, reflecting the ordnance available

In the following year, an artillery company was provided as the basis of a mercenary company for the Dutch army, and was commanded by Hauptmann Schmidtgall. However the company was assigned to the Capregiment. 1789 saw the horse artillery company be increased to 97 men and 54 horses and the staff of the artillery regiment being altered, and reduced to four companies, armed with 4x 6pdr and 4x 3-pdr.

With the outbreak of war in 1792, a provisional artillery company was drawn from the Guard battery, and was commanded by Oberstwachtmeister von Becke. Through continual fighting most of this force was lost.

In June 1800 the artillery was re-organised yet again, a Bombardier company was formed under the command of Oberstleutnant Bausch, it was armed with 6x 2-pdr, and had the following men:
> 1 Lt Colonel, 1 Lieutenant,1 Sergeant, 4 Corporals, 41 gunners, 1 wagon master,1 farrier black smith, 17 drivers.

A second battery was formed, armed with six 6pdrs and two 8pdr howitzers, which was reinforced soon after with the addition of 15 gunners, the formation of a third or depot company and the establishment of an artillery commando armed with eight guns manned by 156 gunners. . In 1800 each foot company had the following equipment:

Number	Equipment
8	4 horse artillery piece (6x 6-pdr, 2x 7-pdr howitzers)
10	2 horse artillery caissons
6	2 horse infantry ammunition wagons
1	2 horse Jager ammunition wagon
1	2 horse field forge
1	4 horse requisition wagon
1	2 horse staff ambulance wagon
1	4 horse light horse staff wagon
2	Pack horses
3	4 horse horse infantry battalion staff wagons
4	Pack horses for the Jagers
15	Pack horses for the infantry
1	3 horse cart for the light infantry
17	4 horse tent wagons
67	Riding horses

The horse artillery was re-formed on 7 June 1801, and was armed with 2x 3-pdr, manned by 1 sergeant, 1 trumpeter, 4 corporals and 60 gunners. Two 6-pdrs were added on 20th August along with the following men and equipment:

> 1 Hauptmann, 1 Lieutenant, 1 Trumpeter, 2 Corporals, 18 mounted gunners, 8 non mounted gunners, 21 riding horses, 16 draft horses, 8 drivers, 1 mounted wagon master.

At the same time, the 3-pdrs were withdrawn and replaced with 6-pdr, two more 6-pdr being added on 19th May 1803, and additional 2x 7-pdr howitzers being added on 11 July of the same year. At the same time an infantry artillery battery was formed, armed with 10x 3-pdr, later increased to 14 on 6th September 1803.

The Duchy of Württemberg joined the French in 1805. As a reward duke Friedrich is crowned as king on 1 January 1806 and the new kingdom joins the Confederation of the Rhine on 12th July 1806 (Treaty of Paris, the federal contingent fixed at 18,000 men). In 1806 the Württemberger artillery consisted of two foot batteries that have six 6pdr guns and four 7pdr howitzers manned by 137 men.

In December 1807, a second Horse Artillery company was raised with the same establishment, and a third foot artillery company. In January 1808 saw the Horse Artillery of the Guard being increased to 72 gunners, a third Horse Artillery company being raised on 24th May 1808.

In 1809, the three existing batteries were reformed as light artillery and a fourth heavy battery was formed, equipped with 3x 12-pdr guns and 2x 7-pdr howitzers manned by 122 men. At the beginning of the 1809 campaign, the foot batteries left two 6-pdr in the arsenal before leaving for active service. Each gun and howitzer was provisioned with 110 rounds and 20 rounds of canister.

On 1st May 1810 the organisation underwent a major re-organisation and now consisted of a staff, three horse companies, and a foot battalion of four companies and the depot company. The organisation being as follows:

1 Artillerie Kommandeur, 2 Kommndeurs (1Horse Artillery 1 Foot Artillery), 1 Adjutant,1 Regimental Quartermaster, 1 Senior Physician, 1 Veterinarian,1 Staff Quartermaster, 1 Provost.

1st and 2nd Horse Artillery:

4x 6-pdr cannon, 2x 7-pdr howitzers,6 Caissons, 1 tool wagon, 1 captain, 1 first lieutenant, 1 second lieutenant, 1 sergeant, 1 quartermaster, 1 senior corporal, 7 corporals, 2 trumpeters, 12 first gunners, 72 gunners, 1 wagon master, 24 train soldiers, 3 craftsmen, 3 officers servants, 32 riding horses, 48 draught horses.

3rd Artillery Company

3x 6-pdr cannon, 1x 7-pdr Howitzer, 4x caissons,1 tool wagon, 1 staff captain,1 second lieutenant, 1 sergeant, 1 quartermaster, 1 senior corporal, 5 corporals, 2 trumpeters, 8 first gunners, 48 gunners, 3 craftsmen, 2 officers servants.

1st, 2nd 3rd Foot Companies

6x 6-pdr cannon, 2x 7-pdr howitzers, 8x caissons,1 captain, 1 first lieutenant, 1 second lieutenant,1 sergeant, 1 quartermaster,1 senior corporal, 9 corporals, 2 drummers, 10 first gunners, 88 gunners, 3 craftsmen.

4th Company:

5x 12-pdr cannon, 2x heavy howitzer, 6x caissons, 2 second lieutenants, 2 sergeants, 112 gunners, 6 craftsmen

In the January of 1810 the 2nd Horse company was reduced to the same organisation as the 3rd horse company. On 2nd December 1810 4x 3-pdr were attached to the Infantry regiment Prinz Frederick. The artillery commando was dispatched on 24th April 1811 to Danzig, and tow months later on 30th June, in preparation for the invasion of Russia, the foot artillery was re-armed and the four companies now had 2x 12-pdr, 2x 6-pdr and 2x 7-pdr howitzer served by 76 gunners.

The war time strength of the Guard Horse Artillery battery and the 3rd Horse Artillery battery was five officers and 155 men, including 34 train soldiers, 34 draught horses and 54 riding horses. The 1st and 2nd Horse batteries along with the Guard Foot Battery consisted of five officers, 155 men, 40 train soldiers, 66 draught horses and two riding horses. The 1st Heavy Foot Battery had four officers, 181 men, three train soldiers, 90 draught horses and 3 riding horses. The 2nd Heavy Foot Battery had four officers, 172 men, 42 train soldiers, 72 draught horses and two riding horses. The 1st and 2nd Light Foot Batteries had four officers, 163 men and 33 train soldiers. The two reserve companies and the arsenal-workmen company had three officers and 130 men, the Gewehrfabrirkbeiter Company had two officers and 128 men.

In May 1814, a 4 gun Guard Foot Artillery company was raised, in addition to this there were two 6 gun light artillery companies and two heavy foot companies armed with 12-pdr. In 1815 the Horse Artillery had four 6-pdr, two 7-pdr howitzers, the light artillery four 6-pdr and two 7-pdr howitzers, and the heavy artillery six 12-pdr with a double ammunition issue

The French looked on Württemberg as military equals, Marshal Ney noting in 1812 that the Horse Artillery was as good as French Horse Artillery, and probably better than some companies.

Horse Artillery.

In 1783 saw the formation of a Horse Artillery company attached to the Ducal Guard, and served 4x 3-pdr. By 1788 it became fully organised and incorporated into the Guard:
> 1 Colonel Sergeant, 1 Staff Captain, 4 Lieutenants, 2 Sergeants, 1 Quartermaster, 8 Corporals, 61 gunners and 8 drivers.

The Horse Artillery was re-formed on 7 June 1801, and was armed with two 3-pdr, manned by 1 sergeant, 1 trumpeter, 4 corporals and 60 gunners. Two 6-pdr were added on 20th August 1801 along with the following men and equipment:
> 1 Hauptmann, 1 Lieutenant, 1 Trumpeter, 2 Corporals, 18 mounted gunners, 8 non mounted gunners, 21 riding horses, 16 draft horses, 8 drivers and 1 mounted wagon master.

At the same time, the 3-pdr were withdrawn and replaced with 6-pdr, two more 6-pdr being added on 19 May 1803 and two 7-pdr howitzers being added on 11 July of the same year. In 1810 the organisation was as follows:

1st and 2nd Horse Artillery Company:

4x 6-pdr cannon, 2x 7-pdr howitzer, 6 Caissons and 1 tool wagon, 1 Hauptmann (Captain), 1 First Lieutenant, 1 Second Lieutenant, 1 Sergeant, 1 Quartermaster, 1 Senior corporal, 7 Corporals, 2 trumpeters, 12 first gunners, 72 gunners, 1 wagon master, 24 train soldiers, 3 craftsmen, 3 officers servants, 32 riding horses, 48 draught horses

3rd Horse Artillery Company

3x 6-pdr cannon, 1x 7-pdr Howitzer with 4 caissons and 1 tool wagon 1 Staff Hauptmann (Captain), 1 Second Lieutenant, 1 Sergeant, 1 Quartermaster, 1 senior corporal, 5 corporals, 2 Trumpeters, 8 first gunners, 48 gunners, 3 craftsmen, 2 officers servants.

Equipment.

The guns used by the Duchy were of Austrian inspired designs, and consisted of 12-pdr, 6-pdr,3-pdr and 7-pdr and 10-pdr howitzers. Prior to 1808 all guns used in the Duchy had to be imported from Ausrtria as there was no foundry, but one was set up at Ludwigsburg to produce ordnance for the Duchy and their rolling stock. Powder mills were established at Rottweil, Tubingen, Neuthgen, Korchen and Menzingen to reduce reliance on imported Austrian powder which was no longer politically expedient.

M1809 system.

In 1809 these Austrian styled guns were augmented with the addition of new Württemberg designed guns principally 12-pdr, 6-pdr and 24-pdr howitzers. The 3-pdrs were placed in the regimental artillery. All rolling stock was made to the new Württemberg system as were all gun carriages for ease of repair. A new ammunition wagon which had half of the cover padded with a seat for the horse artillery was introduced. Two gunners in both foot and horse artillery could ride on the carriage, the top of the tool box being padded, in theory two more could be mounted on the limber, and in the horse artillery the rest of the gun crew were mounted on the caisson. The new Württemberg guns owed a lot of the French AnXI equipment in their design.

Württemberg M1809 12-pdr field gun (E Ehmke).

Württemberg M1809 6-pdr horse artillery gun. (E Ehmke).

Württemberg M1809 wurst ammunition caisson (E Ehmke).

The guns in service in 1812 were a mix of Württemberg(called Austrian by the French) and French, the organisation of the equipment being as follows:

	10e Div	11e Div	25e Div	Parc	Reserve	Total
French						
12-pdr					12	12
6-pdr	10	10				20
5.6inch Howitzer	4	4				8
Austrian equipment						
12-pdr			6			6
6-pdr		14				14
6.4inch Howitzer					4	4
5.6 inch Howitzer			8			8
Spare Carriages						
12-pdr				1	2	3
6-pdr	1	1		4		6
6.4inch Hoiwtzer					1	1
5.6inch Howitzer			1	3		4
Caissons						
12-pdr			18	8	36	62

6pdr	15	15	26	20		76
6.4inch Howitzer				6	12	18
5.6inch Howitzer	8	8	16	10		42
Infantry	16	16	16	21		69
Parc Ammunition			7	1		8
Wagons	4	4	5	7	4	24
Tool wagons				1		1
Pontoons				1		1
Field Forge	2	2	2	5	2	13
	60	60	119	88	73	400

The regimental artillery was equipped with the following:

	10e Div	11 Div	total
Regimental Artillery			
3pdr	8	6	14
3pdr Caissons	8	8	16
Infantry Caissons	11	11	22
Field Forges	4	3	7

The artillery park attached to the Cavalry Corps for the 1812 campaign were as follow:

Equipment	Issued	Munitions used by 5th July 1812	Remaining
6pdr field gun	8		8
24pdr Howitzer	4		4
6pdr Caisson	10		10
24pdr Howitzer Caisson	6		6
Field Forge	1		1

Ammunition Wagon	2		2
6pdr ammunition: coffret use	197	9	188
24pdr Howitzer ammunition	20	0	20
6pdr ammunition drawn from caissons	958	126	832
24pdr howitzer powder charges	298	88	210
	Extant equipment 5th July 1812	Equipment & Munitions at Bromberg 1812	Equipment & Munitions at Wilna November 1812
6pdr cannon and carriage	8	0	0
24pdr Howitzer and carriage	4	0	0
6pdr Caisson	10	6	2
24pdr Howitzer caisson	6	4	2
Infantry Caissons	1	1	1
Replacement 6pdr carriage	0	0	1
Replacement carriage 24pdr howitzer	0	0	1
Ammunition Wagon	1	0	3
Field Forge	1	0	1
6pdr Coffret ammunition	1,500	690	0

6pdr ammunition & ball	300	150	0
24pdr howitzer cartridge & ball	20	12	0
Infantry cartridges	31,460	0	0
24pdr howitzer charges	604	312	0
Powder charges for 24pdr Howitzer	580	324	0
Priming tubes	3,704	1,568	0
Quick match	405	197	0
Slow match (KG)	118	50	0

When the artillery corps was reorganised after the Russian campaign, four horse batteries were formed, equipped with four 6pdr : a Guard horse battery and three foot batteries. The war time strength of the guard horse artillery battery and the 3rd horse artillery battery was five officers and 155 men, including 34 train soldiers, 34 draught horses and 54 riding horses.

The 1st, and 2nd Horse batteries along with the Guard Foot Battery consisted of five officers, 155 men. 40 train soldiers, 66 draught horses and two riding horses. The 1st Heavy Foot Battery had four officers, 181 men, three train soldiers, 90 draught horses and 3 riding horses. The 2nd Heavy Foot Battery had four officers, 172 men, 42 train soldiers, 72 draught horses and two riding horses. The 1st and 2nd Light Foot Batteries had four officers, 163 men and 33 train soldiers.

The two reserve companies and the arsenal-workmen company had three officers and 130 men, the Gewehrfabrirkbeiter company had two officers and 128men.

In May 1814 a 4 gun Guard Foot Artillery company was raised, in addition to this there were two 6 gun light artillery companies and two heavy foot companies armed with 12-pdr. In 1815 the horse artillery had 4x 6-pdr, 2x 7-pdr howitzers, the light artillery 4x 6-pdr and 2x 7-pdr howitzers, and the heavy artillery 6x12-pdr with a double ammunition issue. Battery vehicle organisation in 1815 was 6x 12-pdr or 6-pdr, 2x 10-pdr howitzers, 8 first line caissons, 3 second line caissons, two per gun, and 2 howitzer caissons, one per piece, 2 battery wagons and a field forge a total of 24 vehicles.

The 6x 12-pdr were issued with 693 round shot and 144 canister rounds, six 6-pdrs with 1,056 round shot and 198 canister rounds, two 10-pdr howitzers 164 shells and 40 canister rounds in the caissons, for ready use were 115 roundshot and 24 canister rounds for the 12-pdr on the limbers, 176 roundshot and 33 canister for the 6-pdr and 82 shells and 20 canister for the howitzers. The 12-pdr were drawn by 8 horses, the 6-pdr, howitzer and caissons by 6 horses, the other vehicles by four horses.

The French looked on Württemberg as military equals, Marshal Ney noting in 1812 that the Horse Artillery was as good as French horse artillery, and probably better than some French companies. The artillery was always well equipped and trained.

Ammunition Provision.
Both foot and horse 6-pdr cannon had 94 roundshot and 26 canisters immediately available in limber boxes and ammunition carts. The 12-pdr cannon had 123 roundshot, 40 canister and 12 grape. The howitzer 12 canister and 72 shell in ammunition vehicles. The rest of the ammunition was carried in Reserve Park (on average 130-180 rounds for every gun). New Caissons were introduced in 1813, which carried 1 canister rounds and 74 round shot for a 6-pdr, 6 canister rounds , and 52 roundshot for a 12-pdr and 32 shells and 4 canister rounds for a howitzer. The limber mounted

ammunition box was designed to carry 6 canister rounds and 26 round shot for the 6-pdr, 6 canister rounds and 15 round shot for the 12-pdr and 6 shell and 4 canister for the howitzer. This caisson design replaced the Wursts of 1808 and 1810. They were smaller than their predecessors, could still carry gunners as well as a spare wheel on the back.

Battery Organisation.

A 6-pdr or 12-pdr battery had the following vehicles allocated to it:

    6x 6-pdr, or 12-pdr

    2x 10-pdr howitzer

    8 first line caissons (one per piece)

    3 second line caissons (1 per 2 pieces)

    2 second line howitzer caissons (one per piece)

    2 munition wagons.

    1 forge.

In total 24 horses. A 12-pdr was drawn by 8 horses, a 6-pdr and howitzer by 6 and all other vehicles by 4. A 12-pdr battery had 93 officer, NCO's, gunners and drivers, 8 riding horses, 150 draft horses and 8 spare draft horses; a 6-pdr battery 86 officers, NCOs, and drivers, 7 riding horses, 138 draft horses and 8 spare.

Württemberg 6-pdr gun tube. This design was used prior to the adoption of the M1809 equipment.

Württemberg 7-pdr howitzer gun tube of the type used before 1809.

Glossary1: Organisation

ARMOURER: artillery specialist who was charged with the manufacture, maintenance and repair of weapons (sabres, muskets, bayonets etc).

ARMOURY: A manufacturing or storage facility for arms and *ordnance*.

ARSENAL: A storage facility for *ordnance and ordnance stores*. Some arsenals were also used for the construction and repair of *ordnance* equipment.

ARTIFICER: Military workmen who was responsible for the repair and maintenance of the gun carriages and other items of rolling stock.

ARTILLERY CREW: Military personnel responsible for the maintenance, transportation, and operation of the various *artillery pieces* and the equipment and horses needed to properly support the *battery*. Support personnel included horse drivers, horse holders, and specialized functions such as blacksmiths.

ARTILLERY PARK: 1) A space occupied by animals, wagons, and *artillery* contiguous to a military camp. 2) A collection of one or more *batteries*.

ARTILLERY RESERVE: Designated *batteries* which were to remain *limbered* and hitched, ready to move quickly into position during battle. Their purpose was to replace disabled batteries or to move rapidly where the enemy was massing for an attack.

ARTILLERY: Generic term used to describe the heavy weapons of every description with the *implements* and materials necessary for their use.

BATTERIES: A battery consists of two or more pieces of artillery in the field. The term battery also implies the emplacement of ordnance destined to act offensively or defensively. It also refers to the company charged with a certain number of pieces of ordnance. The ordnance constitutes the battery. Men serve the battery. Horses drag it, and epaulments may shelter it.

BATTERY: A term applied to one or more *pieces* of *artillery*, or to the place where they were positioned. *Batteries*, under the command of a captain, were further broken down into sections. Each section consisted of two *guns* under the command of a lieutenant. One *gun*, along with a *caisson* and *limber*, was designated as a platoon and served under a sergeant and two corporals.

BOMBARDIER: An artilleryman versed in that department of arms which relates especially to bombs and shells, mortars and howitzers, grenades and fuses.

FIELD ARTILLERY: *Artillery piece* designated for use in the field. The essential quality of field artillery was mobility, and it was used in combination with the infantry and cavalry to augment their fire. Field artillery prepared the way for operations by firing at the enemy while he was still out of *range* of other weapons. It also served as a point of support and assembly when troops were driven back.

FIELD BATTERY: A certain number of *pieces* of *artillery* (commonly eight) that operated on the battlefield divided into **foot artillery** and ***horse artillery***.

FIELD PARK: An *artillery* grouping made up of the spare *carriages*, reserved supply of *ammunition*, and the tools and materials for extensive repairs and for making up ammunition for the service of the army in the field. Reserve *batteries* were usually attached to the field park.

FIELD TRAIN: See *Artillery Train.*

FLYING ARTILLERY: See *Horse Artillery.*

FOOT BATTERY:

GUN CREW: See *Artillery Crew.*

GUNNER: The member of an *artillery crew*, usually the sergeant, who was responsible for giving the orders for cleaning, loading, and firing the weapon. The gunner was usually the member who actually fired the weapon.

HORSE ARTILLERY: A highly manoeuvrable *artillery* unit in which all the *cannoneers* were mounted or rode on vehicles. These units were especially adapted for use with cavalry, for sudden attacks upon particular points, and for supporting the advance or covering the retreat of an army.

PARK, Parc: See *Artillery Park.*

PIECE: A generic term which is used to denote any *artillery* weapon.

Glossary 2: Ordnance

BARREL: See *Tube*.

BASE RING: A projecting band of metal that adjoined the base of the *breech*, and was connected to the body of the *gun* by a concave moulding.

BORE DIAMETER: The *cannon* diameter at its muzzle measured from wall to wall in a smoothbore.

BORE LENGTH: The entire length measurement inside the *tube* including the *chamber*, if one was present.

BORE: Includes all the drilled out portion of the *tube* including the *chamber* (if there is one), the *cylinder*, and the conical or spherical surface connecting them with the drilled out section.

BRASS: An alloy composed of copper and zinc and not suitable for *ordnance*.

BREECH: The bottom of a gun tube or chamber.

BRONZE: Copper and tin alloy.

BUSHING: Also called "bushing a *vent*." This was a replacement vent made of metal (normally copper), about 1-inch in diameter, with a hole drilled in the centre. When the ruined or damaged vent was reamed out, the hole was threaded to receive the bushing.

CALIBRE: 1) The diameter of a cannon's *bore* expressed in inches, 2) the inside diameter of a firing *tube*.

CANNON: A general name for large pieces of ordnance or artillery, as distinguished from those pieces that are hand held when fired.

CARRIAGE: see field artillery carriage.

CASCABEL: That part of the *cannon tube* in the rear of the *base ring*. It was composed of the *knob, neck, fillet,* and the base of the *breech*. The cascabel was used to facilitate the handling of the *piece* when mounting and *dismounting*, and when moving it when it was off the *carriage*. Also known as the back weight.

CAST IRON: A hard brittle, impure form of iron obtained by re-melting pig-iron with limestone. It was inflexible, but strong and rugged. Cast iron was used in production of *projectiles*.

CHAMBER: The smaller diameter section of the *bore* near the *breech* of the *gun* that held the *propellant charge* for the *projectile*. A **cylindrical chamber**, shaped as a smaller diameter bore at the bottom of the main bore, was used in howitzers. Its base was rounded or square. A **conical chamber** (also known as a *Gomer chamber* after its inventor), shaped like a frustum of a cone, and was used in *mortars and howitzers*. A **spherical chamber**, a sphere joined by a small diameter cylinder to the bore, was used in early mortars.

CHEEK: The side piece of the *gun carriage* that supported the *trunion*.

DOLPHINS: Two *handles* placed over the centre of gravity of the *piece* in order to assist in mounting or dismounting the piece.

ELEVATING SCREW: Threaded metal cylinder with a four-pronged handle attached to one end. The other end was screwed into the bottom of the *breech*. The gunner would use this screw to elevate or depress the *tube*.

ELEVATION: The vertical angle that the axis of a *gun* or *howitzer* made with the horizon.

FIELD-CARRIAGES: A wooden two wheeled vehicle for the movement of the gun tube in the field. It was formed from two cheeks, separated by horizontal transoms. The carriage had large wheels to increase mobility.

GOMER CHAMBER: See *Chamber.*

HANDLES: See *Dolphins.*

HOWITZER: A short-*barrelled* weapon with a large *powder chamber*. *Howitzers* were lighter and fired *shells* with lower *powder charges* at higher elevations, but lower *ranges* than *guns* of the same calibre.

KNOB: See *Cascabel.*

MANTLET: A bullet-proof shield made of wood, rope matting, or metal used to protect *cannon crews* at the *embrasures.*

MUZZLE: The mouth, or opening, of the *bore* of a *cannon tube* and the face that surrounds it. The muzzle opening was *chamfered*, or bevelled, to prevent abrasion and to facilitate loading.

MUZZLE-LOADER: A weapon which had the *projectile* and *charge* loaded through the mouth, or *muzzle*, of the *bore.*

PIERRIER: A small type of *cannon* or a *mortar* used to throw stones.

PINTLE: An iron pin, with a nut or key at the top, used to anchor the front of the *barbette carriage* to the *pintle plate*. The pintle served as a pivot for the *gun.*

STOCK TRAIL: *Carriage* in which the short *cheeks* supporting the *cannon* were attached to each side of a single central stock.

TRAIL: The part of the stock of the *gun carriage* behind the *cheeks*, or the cheeks that rests on the ground when the *gun* is unlimbered.

TRUCK HANDSPIKE: See *Handspike.*

TRUNIONS: The two short *cylinders* which projected from the sides of a *gun barrel*. These rested on the *cheeks* of the *carriage* and supported the barrel.

TUBE: The correct nomenclature for a *cannon barrel. Tubes* were made of either cast-*iron,* or *bronze.*

VENT: A small hole bored through the *breech* end of the *cannon tube,* into which was placed the fuse.

WINDAGE: The space, or difference, between the bore diameter and the diameter of the projectile.

Bibliography

Primary Sources

Anonymous (1798): "Ueber die reitende Artillerie" Neues Militairisches magazin – Historischen und Scientifischen Inhalts, herausgegeben von Iohann Friedrich Hoyer, 1. Band, 2. Stück Leipzig

Anonymous (1802): Ueber den Gebrauch der reitenden Artillerie" by Von R., in Neues Militairisches magazin – Historischen und Scientifischen Inhalts, herausgegeben von Iohann Friedrich Hoyer, 2. Band, 4. Stück Leipzig

Anonymous (1820) Ueber zwölfpfündige und Haubitz-Batterien, in 'Militair-Wochenblatt' 5. Jahrgang Berlin

Brown R (1795): "An Impartial Journal of a Detachment from the Brigade of Foot Guards, commencing 25 February 1793 and ending 9 May 1795," London

d'Auzon de Boisminart W.P (1840) "Gedenkschriften van den Majoor W.P. d'Auzon de Boisminart - Tijdvak van 1812 – De Veldtocht in Rusland. Gravenhage/Amsterdam 1840

d'Auzon de Boisminart W.P (1848) "Gedenkschriften van den Majoor W.P. d'Auzon de Boisminart Part 2, Tijdvak van 1806-1840 Amsterdam d'Urtubie T.B.S.D. <u>1787 Manual de l'artilleur, contenant tou les objects dont la conaissane ect necessair aux officers et sous officers d'artillerie</u>. Chez Magimal Paris

de Scheel O 1795 <u>Memoires d'Artillerie</u> Chez Magimal Paris

du Teil 2003 <u>The new use of Artillery in Field wars, neccessary knowledge</u>. The Nafziger Collection.

Fave 1854 <u>Emperor Napoleon's New System of Artillery</u>. London

Gassendi J 1801 <u>Aide memoire a l'usage des officers du corps royale de l'artillerie de France attachee au service du terre</u> Chez Magimal Paris

Gassendi J 1819 <u>Aide Memoire a l'usage d'artillerie de France</u> Chez Magimal Paris

Gesseler & Tognarelli 1892: <u>Geschichte des 2 Württembergischen Feldartillerie-regiments Nr. 29, Prinze Luitpold von Bayern.</u> Stuttgart

Gribeauval J B V 1789 <u>Tables de construction de l'artillerie de France</u>. Paris

Griois L 1909 <u>Memoires</u> 1792-1822, Plon-Nourit Paris

Lespinasse A, 1800 <u>Essai sur l'organisation de l'arme de l'artillerie</u>. Paris

Marmont A 1859 De l'esprit des institutions militaries, Paris

Muller H 1873 Die Entwicklung de Feld-Artilleire in Bezug auf Material, Organization und Taktik von 1815 bis 1870. Berlin

Rostaign 1786 Aide Memoire a l'usage des Bouches de Feu Chez Magimal Paris

Rostaign 1792 Manuel du Cannonier Chez Magimal, Paris

Schels, Johann Baptist von 1813: Leichte Truppen; Kleiner Krieg. Ein praktisches Handbuch für Offiziere aller Waffengattungen, 1. Band, 2. Abtheilung Wien

Stuck von Weissenbach 1882: Geschite der Koniglich Württembergischen artillerie Stuttgart.

Tousard L 1809: American Artillerists Companion

van Es, N.J.A.P.H 1898 "Het Historisch Museum van het Korps Rijdende Artillerie" Volume I (Arnhem 1898)

van Sypesteijn Jhr J W 1852 "Geschiedenis van het Regiment Nederlandse Rijdende Artillerie" Zaltbommel

Von Porbeck 1802: Feldzug der Verbündeten in Braband und Flandern 1793, in Hoyer's 'Neues Militairische Magazin' 2. Band, 5. Stück Leipzig

Secondary Sources

Ballada A 1987 Dessins des bouches de feu et construction de l'artillerie d'apres l'arrete du floreal An XI. SHAT

Beck F 1912 <u>Geschite des Grobherzoglich Hessichen Feldartillerie-reglements</u>. Berlin

Bonaparte N 1821 Notes on Artillery cited in The Artillery Revue 1897 VOL. XXIV.

Brieussel Capt. Historique du 3e Regiment d'Artillerie Macon; 1901

Brunet M A 1842 Historie General de l'artillerie Paris, Anselin

Buat E 1911 L'artillerie de campagne. Son histoire, son evolution, son etat actuel Paris, Alcan

Chaleat J 1933 Histoire Technique de l'artillerie de terre en France pendant un siecle (1816-1919) Imprimere Nationale, Paris

Clement Lt. 1890 Historique du 4e Regiment d'Artillerie;

Compaana J 1901 L'artillerie en campagne 1792-1901. Paris, Berge-Levrault.

Fave I 1845 Histoire et tactique de trios armes et pus particularment de l'artilleire de compagne. Paris

Fave 1862 Etudes sur le passé et l'avenir l'artillerie J Dumaine, Paris

Fave I 1871 Etudes sur le pase et l'avenir de l'artillerie tome V, Paris

Hennebert E 1887 L'artillerie Paris

Historique du 2e Regiment d'Artillerie. Grenoble; 1899

Historique des Corps de Troupes de l'Armee Francaise Paris; 1900

Hughes, 1969 British Smooth Bore Artillery, the Muzzle loading artillery of the 18th and 19th centuries. London

Jomini 1862 The Art of War translated by Capt. G H Mendell and Lt W P Craighill 1971 Greenwood Press, Conneticut

Massin J and Brisson E 1980 Notices Biographes sur les principaux personages de l'epoque Napoleonienne, Paris.

Laurema M 1956 L'artillerie de compagne francaise pednant les gueres de la revolution Helsinki

Martinien A.1899 Tableaux par Corps et par Batailles des Officiers tues et blesse pendant les guerres de l'Empire 1805-1815 Paris.

Mullie M.C. 1851 Biographie des Celebrites militaires des Armes de Terre et de Mer 2 Vols Paris.

Roberts J 1863 The hand book of artillery for the service of the United Sates (army and militia) with the manual of heavy artillery, including that of the new iron carriage. New York

Schwertfeger, B (1901) Geschichte der Königlich Deutschen Legion 1803 - 1816 2 vols (Hannover and Leipzig.

Suzane 1874 Histoire de l'artillerie Francaise, Hetzel, Paris

Taenzer M A (nd) The Organisation of the King's German Legion Artillery 1814 to 1815 in The Napoleon Series

Von Hartmann, Sir Georg Julius (1901): Der Königlich Hannoversche General Sir Julius v. Hartmann Berlin

Von Reitzenstein, J. Frhr (1900) Das Geschützwesen und die Artillerie in den Landen Braunschweig und Hannover von der ersten Anwendung eines Pulvergeschützes 1365 bis auf die Gegenwart 3 vols Leipzig

V. Sichart (1866 – 1898) Geschichte der Königlich Hannoverschen Armee 5 vols Hannover and Leipzig

Quintin D. and B. Dictionnaire des Colonels de Napoleon Paris; 1996.

Tertiary Sources

Alder K 1997 Engineering the Revolution: Arms and Enlightenment in France 1763-1815. Princeton

Chartrand R Napoleon's Guns (vol 1 + 2) Osprey Publications.

Douglas, H. 1832 An Essay on the Principles and Construction of Military Bridges and the Passage of Rivers in Military Operations 2nd edition; London : Thomas and William Boone pp183 - 191

Falk S L 1964 Artillery for the Land Service: The development of a System in Military Affairs Vol, 28 pp97-110

Gillispie C C and Alder 1998 Engineering the Revolution in Technology and Culture Vol 39 No. 4 pp733-754

Graves D 1984 De Scheels treatise on Artillery Museum Restoration Service Bloomfield

McConachy B 2001 The Roots of Artillery Doctrine: Napoleonic Artillery Tactics Reconsidered in The Journal of Military History Vol 65 No. 3 pp617-640

Quimby, R 1957. The Background of Napoleonic Warfare New York : Columbia University Press; 1957.

van Uythoven, G 1999: "Voorwaarts Bataven!" Zaltbommel 1999

www.ingramcontent.com/pod-product-compliance
Lightning Source LLC
Chambersburg PA
CBHW070314240426
43663CB00038BA/2279